When Teardrops Dance

Can We Really Rejoice in Our Suffering?

June Lewers Terry

Fleming H. Revell
A Division of Baker Book House Co
Grand Rapids, Michigan 49516

© 1994 by June Lewers Terry

Published by Fleming H. Revell
a division of Baker Book House Company
P.O. Box 6287, Grand Rapids, MI 49516-6287

Printed in the United States of America

Library of Congress Cataloging-in-Publication Data

Terry, June Lewers.
    When teardrops dance: can we really rejoice in our suffering? / June Lewers Terry.
    p. cm.
    ISBN 0-8007-5510-3
    1. Suffering—Religious aspects—Christianity. 2. Hope—Religious as-pects—Christianity. 3. Suffering—Biblical teaching. 4. Hope—Biblical teaching. 5. Bible. N.T. Romans—Devotional literature. 6. Terry, June Lewers. I. Title.
BT732.7.T47 1994
231'.8—dc20   93-33905

Unless otherwise indicated, Scripture taken from the HOLY BIBLE, NEW IN-TERNATIONAL VERSION®. NIV®. Copyright © 1973, 1978, 1984 by Inter-national Bible Society. Used by permission of Zondervan Publishing House. All rights reserved.

*When
Teardrops
Dance*

For Jim
and
for Ruth

In memory of my father,
Donald Guillette Lewers

And with solid hope for South Africa

Contents

Foreword

We live in a culture that doesn't know how to suffer. We grow up thinking that if we are good we won't suffer; or that if we raise our standard of living sufficiently we won't suffer; or that if we acquire an education we will be smart enough not to suffer. If suffering rudely intrudes anyway, we call for anesthesia. Anesthesia, which is most useful on occasions of surgery, is most harmful in matters of soul.

Despite (could it be because of?) our vaunted affluence and learning, we men and women of North America seem for the most part to be scandalously ignorant with regard to human suffering. More scandalous still, a great many Christians are currently complicitous in this ignorance. Christians right and left, Christians whose identifying symbol is the cross of Jesus and whose vocation is determined by that same cross, are abandoning it for careers in anesthesiology.

This is a scandal because Christians are the world's experts on suffering. The world deserves to know what we know about suffering, it *needs* to know what we have learned from Jesus at the cross of Jesus. The people in our neighborhoods need to know that suffering is not the worst thing that can happen to them, that oblivion is not preferable to suffering.

June Terry intends to help us recover the wise and bold response to suffering that is at the center of the Christian gospel. She refuses to go along with the cultural trends, whether secular or religious, plants her feet firmly and joyfully in Holy Scripture and the community that reads it believingly, faces the huge fact of human suffering, and gives witness to the consequences, consequences far preferable to anesthesia.

This is mature Christian writing. After reading only a few pages we realize that these paragraphs have a "lived through" quality to them. There is no condescending advice-giving here, there are no cheerful adolescent pep talks, no detached and impersonal explanations. Suffering has gone into the writing, but not *just* suffering, *Christian* suffering, suffering that has wrestled with the angel. The robust liveliness in and between the lines is evidence of the maturity in Christ and the cross that provides the rest of us access to Christian wisdom.

What is just as important but not as immediately obvious is that this is scholarly work. June Terry is a competent Greek scholar and uses her exegetical knowledge of St. Paul's letter to the Romans deftly. But there is not a hint of pedantry here. All the scholarship is hidden. It is hidden in the way a foundation is hidden, accessible if we look for it, but otherwise simply there, providing a reassuring, dependable, and stable base for constructing a life. What she writes, though confirmed in her experience, doesn't originate there—it all comes out of an exact reading of God's revelation in Holy Scripture.

Christians who ignore or forget or avoid suffering, who never allow suffering to take them to the specifically Christian depths of love and hope that have been revealed in our Scriptures and continue to be validated by our brothers and sisters in Christ, are no match for the wiles of the devil. In an age like ours, when we urgently need all the mature Christians we can get, we cannot afford to let spiritual immaturity go unremarked or unchallenged in our ranks. For very strategic reasons, then, I count *When Teardrops Dance* as required reading.

Eugene H. Peterson

Acknowledgments

During the Olympics a few years ago, a commercial pictured an exhausted runner, struggling to complete a fictional race and collapsing flat on the finish line. His wife cheers wildly in the grandstands; then the camera pans the scene, and we see that she alone waits to wave him in, the race long over. Staggering toward publication for six years, I have felt like that; but I could spot a crowd of our patient friends surrounding Jim, my husband.

Three cheers to those who peopled my stadium: to my stepmother, Rachel; to my niece, Debbie Lewers; to Jim's daughter, Rebecca; to Cyndi Bergman, Kim Palmer, Teresa Dunn, Steven Hines, Hope Eddy, Faye Hansen, Bill Graddy, Esther Wiens, and Sister Harriet Schnurr; and to Jan Aucompaugh, who checked details in England for accuracy.

My lively thanks to others who have believed in me and have run alongside for years. They are June Salstrom, Joan Carter, Margi Hollingshead, Betty Fowler, Abe and Verleen Baerg, the Baptista family, Anna, Bob, and Carol Rose, Harvey and Naomi Bostrom. I am unable to credit sufficiently my parents, Guillette and Iva Lewers, and my kindred-friends of thirty years, Mary and Stan Hoffman.

In addition to recognizing the New Testament Department at Trinity Evangelical Divinity School, in particular Drs. Moo, Liefeld, and Carson, I am grateful to Ken Kantzer for his wise counsel and encouragement. And how can I describe Eugene and Jan Peterson's graciousness? He kept me upright and on course; without their support, I would have decided a few laps were plenty!

Beryl Bevan, a joyful toast to you for arriving from South Africa in time for dinner at the Coyote Riverhouse where we celebrated publication, and for giving us the weeks that enclosed the evening.

To Ruth McKellin, applause and a medal for being there at every turn. As my confidant, consultant, and cheerleader, Ruth called forth a part of the application of Paul's writing to contemporary life, while progressing through her own grief.

Gratitude and a smart salute to Joanne Gerber, for superb editing here in Canada, and to Bill Petersen, Mary Suggs, and Jan Ortiz at Revell.

And Jim, faithful companion, patient partner, creative humorist, sustaining strength, resident editor, computer teacher: thank you.

To God: glory and deep thanksgiving!

Romans 5:1–11

[1]Therefore, since we have been justified through faith, we have peace with God through our Lord Jesus Christ, [2]through whom we have gained access by faith into this grace in which we now stand. And we rejoice in the hope of the glory of God. [3]Not only so, but we also rejoice in our sufferings, because we know that suffering produces perseverance; [4]perseverance, character; and character, hope. [5]And hope does not disappoint us, because God has poured out his love into our hearts by the Holy Spirit, whom he has given us. [6]You see, at just the right time, when we were still powerless, Christ died for the ungodly. [7]Very rarely will anyone die for a righteous man, though for a good man someone might possibly dare to die. [8]But God demonstrates his own love for us in this: While we were still sinners, Christ died for us. [9]Since we have now been justified by his blood, how much more shall we be saved from God's wrath through him! [10]For if, when we were God's enemies, we were reconciled to him through the death of his Son, how much more, having been reconciled, shall we be saved through his life! [11]Not only is this so, but we also rejoice in God through our Lord Jesus Christ, through whom we have now received reconciliation.

Romans 8:18–30

[18]I consider that our present sufferings are not worth comparing with the glory that will be revealed in us. [19]The creation waits in eager expectation for the sons of God to be revealed. [20]For the creation was subjected to frustration, not by its own choice, but by the will of the one who subjected it, in hope [21]that the creation itself will be liberated from its bondage to decay and brought into the glorious freedom of the children of God. [22]We know that the whole creation has been groaning as in the pains of childbirth right up to the present time. [23]Not only so, but we ourselves, who have the firstfruits of the Spirit, groan inwardly as we wait eagerly, for our adoption as sons, the redemption of our bodies. [24]For in this hope we were saved. But hope that is seen is no hope at all. Who hopes for what he already has? [25]But if we hope for what we do not yet have, we wait for it patiently. [26]In the same way, the Spirit helps us in our weakness. We do not know what we ought to pray, but the Spirit himself intercedes for us with groans that words cannot express. [27]And he who searches our hearts knows the mind of the Spirit, because the Spirit intercedes for the saints in accordance with God's will. [28]And we know that in all things God works for the good of those who love him, who have been called according to his purpose. [29]For those God foreknew he also predestined to be conformed to the likeness of his Son, that he might be the firstborn among many brothers. [30]And those he predestined, he also called; those he called, he also justified; those he justified, he also glorified.

Introduction

Romans 5 has long enticed me, so that I can say I have been intrigued, romanced, and overwhelmed by it. I have surrendered to it. I am at home and comfortable with it.

I remember as a twenty-one-year-old nurse being startled to read in Romans that suffering could produce hope. I remember that I wrote poems about pain and its consequences and was fascinated by the fact that softly radiant pearls begin to form when bits of sand irritate oysters inside their gnarled, apparently misshapen shells.

Then at twenty-six, I became a missionary in South Africa. I taught nursing to Zulu women; stood with them at bedsides where patients gasped for oxygen, where children died because of prolonged hunger and contaminated water. My own heart sank at the severity of their distresses. The suffering theme simmered. At that time in South Africa, blacks were defined by what they were not. They were not white; I was. And I sensed also the struggles of my white South African friends who handled the racial issue at varying levels of awareness. Having many black friends as well as white friends, I walked the tightrope of apartheid and jumped off it regularly to enjoy those I loved on either side. All these friends were hurting, and I hurt with them.

Back in the United States at age thirty-eight, and while attending seminary, I began an exploration, reserving four summers for the study of Romans 5: "We rejoice in our sufferings, because we know. . . ." Because we know what? The passage drew me and held me. I could not let it go, nor would the truth release me. That was as I wanted it.

During my time at the seminary, Michelle, my good friend and a committed Christian, grabbed a butcher knife and tried to kill her mother and herself. The phone rang and the worried voice of her pastor reported the attempted murder and suicide. I had heard depression in her flattened voice and had known that she was receiving professional counsel. But Michelle, now in a prison hospital, was suffering. Where was hope? At first it was not visible. After several months, though, and with the encouragement of counselor, friends, and church, Michelle grew into health again. During this time I had been taking in Michelle's experience and Romans simultaneously.

North American young people had captured my attention, and as I worked on campus, many of them told me of their growing pains. Not as exotic perhaps as the struggles of faraway people with strange-sounding names, but their hurts were real. Real life, whether African or American, has been for me a laboratory in which to study suffering and hope. Real pain, whether someone else's or my own, has kept my heart tender and my eyes moist. Real truth has carried me through lonely times and childless years. Now at age fifty-two, I have lived with suffering and hope, in one degree of intimacy or another, for almost thirty years. You hold in your hands the fruit of that union.

A remarkable phenomenon: our producing such fruit. Yet in the daily Christian life, it is our task, yours and mine. I am reminded of my returning home from a Monday evening piano lesson as a teenager and saying to my startled mother, "Oh,

Mother, I'm learning to play a Chopin prelude that I'm unworthy to touch!" I held up my hands, turning them to look with astonishment that they would attempt to interpret anything so-far-beyond-description beautiful. And as I look back now I wonder if Mother rolled her eyes skyward, questioning where I'd come from. Such teenage drama is middle-aged appropriate, for as I look at this Scripture, I am small to have interacted with it, yet I am exhilarated by its truth. I have been unable to walk away from it unreceptive and unmingled. So, Romans and I have experienced a blessed union, a sanctified merger.

What can Scripture tell me for real life, for contemporary difficulties? What can Scripture tell me about the difficulties of Karen and Steve and Rev. Mac, whose extraordinary stories I am about to tell you? They are real people who actually have had all the problems I am about to describe. Like most others whose stories I tell, I have changed their names, but I have not put words in their mouths for the purpose of illustrating truth.

What about suffering that is less striking than Karen's progressive disease, or the child abuse Steve endured, or Rev. Mac's suicide? What about the man who drags to work each day, on the edge of burnout but committed to his job because, among other reasons, his family needs to eat? What about the teacher who wears herself out trying to be fair on every report card, seeing lists of grades on the ceiling as she lies awake at night? What about the single parent with a sick or disabled child? Or, what about the college student who has an aching self-concept but is matched with a hypercritical roommate? How does this suffering connect with biblical hope?

Is it possible to *rejoice* in suffering as Paul seems to expect? If so, how? Where is square one? How does one begin such an unlikely exercise as *rejoicing* in one's struggles?

Once we have explored the answers to these questions, will you and I begin to indulge in an intolerable distortion of "rejoicing" in a friend's dire diagnosis or another's job loss?

> The toad beneath the harrow knows
> Exactly where each toothpoint goes;
> The butterfly upon the road
> Preaches contentment to that toad.
>   Rudyard Kipling

Will we start preaching contentment to those who are experiencing pain worse than ours? Will we engage in butterfly-flitting while a toad feels the harrow? Horrors!

Our careful study of what Paul has written will prevent our twisting the truth, but in order to understand him we must agree together to shelve our own preconceived notions. We must dig for truth and answers. Along the way we'll encounter more questions. Suffering produces patience, character, and hope. Hope for what? Hope for relief? Hope for something even better? Is this hope a compensation for suffering, or is it more than that? Does hope grow out of suffering just as a plant grows from a seed?

Isn't there an easier way to know Christ than in the fellowship of suffering that Paul describes? Isn't there an easier way to explore the nature of God? Isn't there some way that is less time-consuming? Isn't there some way that is just plain less consuming?

And if suffering does indeed produce patience, is it the kind of patience that looks like resignation, sitting still with a sweet plastic smile and folded hands? And how can something as dark as suffering actually *produce* something as bright as hope? Isn't there any other way to find hope?

To get at the answers to these questions I will look at experience. And to get a full picture, seen from many angles, viewed from God's perspective, I must treat the Bible like a diamond mine, chipping out stones that need to be cut and polished until I am sure of the truth. I'll tunnel into Romans

5 from a wider context; seeing what Paul is discussing in this section of Romans and checking for his purpose in writing the entire book. I'll ask: What does he say elsewhere in the New Testament about suffering and rejoicing? What do other New Testament authors have to say about it?

Whoever said that we mustn't judge a book by its cover probably meant that we should examine the contents. How about examining the author, too, looking quite closely at him and his life? You and I may accept Paul's writing because of our high view of Scripture, but it is vital also to see Paul as a mature Christian man who had more than a nodding acquaintance with God, a harrowed person who knew very well what suffering was all about.

~

Rounding a corner just in time, author Annie Dillard watched a mockingbird's breathtaking free-fall. She had nearly missed the sight by her tardy arrival. Early in *Pilgrim at Tinker Creek*, she writes, "Beauty and grace are performed whether or not we . . . sense them. The least we can do is try to be there." So it is with the beauty and grace of all truth, and of this particular truth: *Suffering creates hope*. The least we can do is try to "be there"—to try to begin to understand.

Rhythms
in Real Life

Our tribulation, without ceasing to be tribulation or to be felt to be tribulation, is transformed . . . no longer a passive, dangerous, poisonous, destructive tribulation and perplexity. [Our suffering can be] transformed into a tribulation and perplexity which are creative, fruitful, powerful, promising.

Karl Barth

Biblical hope is entirely realistic: it reckons with the worst.

C. F. D. Moule

1

Test Cases for Truth

"But I want to know God *as he truly is,* not as life super-ficially presents him!" Karen had my full attention and held it with her comment and her deep emotional intensity. Her extreme suffering magnetized her words for all of us. In those days Karen sat in a class I was teaching at a Canadian col-lege and seminary on "Suffering and Hope in Christian Ex-perience." She already had credentials way beyond a college diploma for such a course, for she had endured much greater difficulty than the rest of us who were in the classroom that day. Years younger than I, she surpassed me in the survival of physical and emotional distresses, many of them connected to her multiple sclerosis.

When I think about Annie Dillard's words, "grace tangled in a rapture with violence," I am reminded of Karen. Vio-lence tied to a rapturous grace: the odd juxtaposition came at the sight of a hundred sharks silhouetted in translucent waves against late afternoon sunlight.[1] Karen's life is evidence of God's grace wrapped around the stark violence of disability and its repercussions.

I taught that class with Karen as my student in 1985. Now she lives at some distance. Still, the mail and the telephone bring me news as she outlives crisis after crisis, crying out for God to transform her struggles; for God to clarify her focus on him. Not long ago her husband had the possibility of a cancer diagnosis erased, while Karen awaited surgery for a condition unrelated to multiple sclerosis. She has recently been discharged from the hospital after a serious case of meningitis, and in her thirties, has lost some vision in each eye so that she now sees the world in a "greyish-black snow flurry."

But Karen writes of what she calls "irrevocable hope" in the middle of it all, and says

> My earthenness is so apparent much of the time that I can scarcely pray beyond "Keep the panic at bay . . . help me cope with this minute, this child, this meal." I don't think this is defeat because I am not leaving God out. It is more like total reliance. Sometimes all I can do is trust his written word, but I do trust.

Karen trusts. Sometimes only feebly, but she does trust. Karen is waiting on God to have destructive perplexity transformed into a kind of suffering that is fruitful and promising. She is steeped in biblical truth with an inner 20/20 vision. Her focus is sometimes quite waveringly human, but she eventually returns to look at God. She says in many different ways that she is determined to view God as he truly is, as he is presented in his word.

She reminds me of a South African flower, the protea, which blooms after being charred by fire. Honestly admitting to very bleak times, times of great physical and spiritual weakness, Karen does not renounce God. Her trust, humanly so slight as to be microscopic, has in it a tiny seed that can grow into great joy.

Her trust is rooted in painful reality. Karen is not writing in a glib, easy manner. She does not trivialize her suffering with false or cheap hope, but neither does she divorce her pain from hope, in resignation or in tragic despair.[2]

Karen hurts more than any of us know, but she is being renewed inwardly and is supported by a network of believing friends. With authenticity and shaky faith Karen cries, "I want to know God as he truly is, not just as *life* superficially presents him. I admit I am hurting. I need the help of friends and church." Karen looks at us, those whom she can see. She looks beyond us to focus on the unseen. In suffering, she tries to understand God as he truly is. Her hundreds of shark-toothed pains are not endured in absolute darkness; her most personal hurts are somehow related to waves of shining grace.

Karen's life is a test case for the truth that suffering creates hope. Karen, a mature woman managing present tense problems with ancient truth, has that particular truth in common with Steve, a young man handling past tense abuse.

In the months when Karen and I were becoming acquainted, I was also working in student development and spent hours listening to Steve, a tall, slender fellow of twenty years, with light hair, honest, but pained eyes, and sometimes a boyish grin.

One day as I sat talking with Steve, I inwardly begged God for a parachute-drop of immediate wisdom. I was angry at Steve's father whom I had never met. Steve was describing how his dad had belittled him—abused him with ugly words, big hands, and strong arms. His father had thrown a seven-year-old Steve across a room where he crashed into a piano.

I don't remember what I specifically said to Steve. I recall that God gave me the wisdom to help him; that there were answers on numerous afternoons for Steve; and that most of them he found for himself as I stood by. Steve was

endearing—a person with a cave-in where his self-confidence
should have been, a worried frown taking turns with an uncertain smile, and a great volume of stored-up pain where I
longed to see ease. That was Steve in 1985.

Today, as youth minister in his church, Steve enjoys a fresh
confidence in God and a healthy brand of self-reliance. A
grin less shy and more steady, he has broken his frowning
habit. Has his pain completely been replaced by ease? No,
but an enormous amount of hope and strength have begun
to brighten his thoughts and emotions. Steve is like a delightful greenhouse where growth is obvious in both great
spurts and in long, steady progressions. He knows God more
intimately now than he did even a year ago. Steve is another
test case for suffering and hope.

What happened in Karen and Steve? How did they grow
head and shoulders above others who are stunted in bitterness or stuck in self-pity? Because they are Christians, you
say? Isn't that only a part of the answer?

Yes, both Steve and Karen are Christians; committed to
Christ, intelligent, searching. Steve, welcome at my door, hope
edging out his frown; Karen, even in her struggles, refreshes
me. Romans shows the fork in the road between the open
route taken by Karen and Steve and the other route overgrown
with the roots of bitterness; a road that trips its travelers.

Young in hope, Karen and Steve have begun to discover
God's unlimited understanding.

> Those that are broken in their hearts,
>   and grieved in their minds,
> He healeth, and their painful wounds
>   He tenderly upbinds.[3]
>   Psalm 147:3

This verse, penned in beautiful calligraphy by a friend,
hangs on our guest-room wall. Its old-fashioned language
presents permanent truth. Karen and Steve are learning its

reality, standing as test cases for the promise of suffering that produces hope.

Consider again the promise of hope and inward healing written by Paul. Doesn't he, too, have impeccable credentials to instruct us on such a promise? At times stressed, perplexed, persecuted, and struck down, Paul says that suffering creates hope and glory (2 Cor. 4:8–9). Paul's life proved the truth even while he wrote it down. Five times Paul endured the lash; three times he was beaten with rods; three times he was shipwrecked. This list of "Dangers Survived" is only the beginning, however, because he also felt the demands placed on him by numerous churches, as well as being a partner in many relationships with all the ups and downs that they include (2 Cor. 11:21–33).[4]

Since God cared for Paul, and since God cares for Karen and Steve, then doesn't he care for me when I, in pain, am going down for the third time?

And if I answer "Yes, oh, yes, he can hold my head above water," then why not my friend, Rev. Mac's? A Christian full grown in grace and well practiced in suffering on the open route to hope, he committed suicide.

2

Unexpected Exit, Unbroken Hope

"I cannot face drawn out deterioration. I just cannot."
When the Reverend Charles Ian MacPherson chose suicide
as a way out, he struggled against Christ, his willing Rescuer.
He seemed to have lost the hope that he had known so well,
and in doing so, left all of us in the church baffled. I know I
cannot sort it all out, but still I ponder his life and death, an
exit I did not expect.

Convinced believer, spiritual example, clear communica-
tor, and vibrant preacher in a suburban church, Rev. Mac
was diagnosed with a fatal kidney disease. Within weeks he
took his own life. The two extremes of his respected character and his grievous choice could not have been greater.

Charles MacPherson was not just anyone. He was the sort
of Christian whose life affected many lives for good. Rev.
Mac, who preached convincingly that suffering creates hope,

died in what some might call a hopeless way. His glad life
and sad death seem impossible to connect; fifty years of convictions refuse to match up with his last choice. His suicide
became the epicenter for many faith-quakes.

I learned of his death just as I was completing this book;
or rather, as I thought I was completing it. But suddenly,
how could I mail the manuscript to the publisher without
looking again at the truth of Romans and the fact of this particular man's death? He was a leader, a preacher. I want to
summarize the issues surrounding his death, along with the
reasons that continue to support my ongoing ownership of
the truth: Suffering can create hope.

I felt angry. Of course, I didn't admit anger at first, but I
was rapidly coming to a boil on a secret burner. Silently I
asked, "Who are you, Rev. Mac, to take life? The *Lord* gives
and takes away." I was upset that he would cause such a burden of grief, guilt, shame, and confusion for his family, and
for many in the church, some of whom were my own friends.
His death sent us reeling. Thoughts bounced around my own
mind faster than I could sort them. Having the breath
knocked out of me, I sat immobilized after the bad news
came; trying to understand; grieving.

A man who had emphasized the goal of finishing well had
intentionally killed himself. Standing together in worship ser-
vices, he had led us in singing, "Oh, Jesus, I have promised
to serve Thee till the end." *This* kind of end?

I still have many questions and few answers. But one thing
helps my compassion for Rev. Mac grow: He shared in our
congregation's attempt to keep weaknesses and fears hidden. You see, we were not as real as Karen. Oh, yes, we as a
community opened ourselves a bit, but what if Rev. Mac had
felt free throughout his adult years to be known more per-
sonally by friends, church members, and staff? What if we
all had given one another more freedom to be fallible human
beings? What if we hadn't denied our fears, if we'd been

more open with at least a few supportive friends? Instead we were self-contained.

In the years preceding his illness, we failed him, in not expecting, encouraging, and accepting expressions of weakness. We wanted our professional Christian leader, our pastor, to be inhumanly perfect. By the time Rev. Mac's illness became symptomatic it was perhaps too late for established privacy to be changed. We should have been there. We should have been present and involved throughout the years. We should not have allowed one another to deny our humanity by sweeping negative emotions under personal carpets. We should not have built barriers that made fears inadmissible so that they remained "unspoken prayer requests." Somehow, we must now let Rev. Mac teach us to become more vulnerable, more open, more transparent, more accepting. We must change habits of inaccessability that allow a buildup of unbearable emotion. Isn't it possible to admit a heavy heart and, all at the same time, possess the faith that suffering creates hope?

Our pastor and friend, through his death, has shown us an unwelcome lesson. We must be accountable to one another, to be honest about feelings and failures, first with one or two friends and then risking more with even more friends. Will this place soiled laundry all over the landscape? No. We can find a balance between allowing privacy and expecting intimacy and closeness with a group of believers who support one another. "Two are better than one, . . . If one falls down, his friend can help him up" (Eccl. 4:9–10).

We expected you to always be here, didn't we, Rev. Mac? Shout from heaven now. Tell us how to change. Remind us that no believer dies a hopeless death. But we must work without your voice to grasp the extent of Christian hope and redefine true victory. We don't expect all the answers (or do we?). Lacking sufficient insight into you and your terror at the thought of slowly dying, we will do as you asked in your final computer file. We will exercise compassion by God's grace. We will consciously set judging aside.

Dying in pardonable sin, Rev. Mac left here still standing in grace, saved through the power of Christ's indestructible life (Rom. 5:1; Heb. 7:16). His lack of *feeling* peace and hope did not affect the *certainty* or *actuality* of hope and peace with Christ.[1] In fact, expectations of escape into Christ's presence may have worked against him at the end.

Perhaps temporarily blinded to his own value as a living person made in God's image, blinded to the fact that suffering is a process that ends in hope at *God's* time, Rev. Mac saw only grace, mercy, peace, and rest. Satan used Scripture against Christ in the temptation (Matt. 4:1–11); why not against this twentieth-century believer? If this was the case, even this apparently successful trick played on a pastor failed. Yes, Rev. Mac died, but he died in Christ. He died, saved by the power of the gospel.

Such foundational truth did little for our emotions at first. I felt as if a long-time player on my football team had not just unintentionally fumbled, but had purposefully come to a screeching halt at the one-yard line, had turned and handed the opposing team the ball, then had walked off the field alone, eyes toward the ground. First-string players just don't do that.

Then a friend said to me, "Even the righteous sin" (Eccl. 7:20). I realized then that I could tolerate quiet private sins all too well—for example, my own pride or envy—but that I expected leaders to be perfect. I did not want to know the sins of my Christian leader, but correct theology taught me that sins were there. I finally had to admit that Rev. Mac was a sinner too, a human being.

Must we each accept that we are sinners *to the end*? Somewhere along the line, couldn't you and I and the pastor get past major public sin? Couldn't we as believers be transformed into Christ's image and still walk on the earth? I had

to admit the answer is no. We are redeemed, but we are redeemed sinners.

You and I know that; we who knew Rev. Mac now know
it more deeply. Yes, suffering does create hope, it does focus
us on God, and it is nothing when compared to glory in
heaven, but we are *not yet* there. We know that even this suicide can be worked for good in God's hands, but we do not
yet know how that can be. We are all caught in the "not yet."

Rev. Mac's choice was shattering, but it reminded us to
shake off our illusions. There is a healthy sort of disillusion-
ment when we have fewer delusions about humanity, fewer
pretenses about ourselves. Only then are we free to expect
perfection of God.

Along with all my feelings and thoughts because of this
death comes fear, fear at the realization that suicide can be
committed by Christians who have been faithful. I want assurance that this cannot be. But I recognize again that God
gives us freedom to choose. He does not give us a set of
failure-proof formulas. He gives us a book full of answers,
yet not all the answers.

Those of us who are evangelicals want all the answers. We
believe that Christ is the answer; and he is. Flowing from this
center are many solutions. Satisfaction with these answers
obscures the fact that we are missing some pieces of life's
puzzles. We forget that only God has them all. Pastor in his
absence is teaching me the acceptability of vagueness, of
blank spaces where I expect neat answers to fit into place.
My response to God's silence, my acceptance of mystery, my
tolerance for ambiguity is a part of fidelity, faith in the black
hours when the music seems flat and dull. Faith fuels the
courage of not knowing.

I am more comfortable with this silence than I would have
expected for two reasons: As my faith in God grows I handle uncertainty a bit better, and I've noticed recently how
Christians who *appear* to have all the answers repel others.

I don't want their answers of cheap optimism, but I do know the answers of deep, true, biblical hope.

> Optimism is in reality the mimic of hope in that it expects something good to happen. It is unlike hope in that it is a way of relating to the world that misses the ambiguity and fails to consider its evil and negative features. Consequently it appears as arrogant, brash, complacent or insensitive . . . [It can come] in pious Christian dress. It uses all the right phrases and . . . an answer for everything, but a "theology that has a prefabricated answer for everything is unbearable."[2]

To prevent my use of prefabricated answers, I need particular events and experiences that carry thick question marks. This list of things that are beyond me does something healthy inside to keep me real, to help me stay in touch with the world, especially with nonbelievers who are muddled and lost without Christ.

So, I learn. I am learning to forgive you, Rev. Mac, absent friend. I choose to forgive you though I understand so little. Such forgiveness is a foundation for further understanding.

A friend told me recently that Rev. Mac had always seen some good in euthanasia or mercy killing. This helps me understand a little about how he may have rationalized his decision. Quick suicide instead of prolonged disease. Friends who saw him in the days before his death describe an uncharacteristic vacancy and depression. He seemed to retreat from earthly life in small stages before the last day. His illness had wreaked havoc on his body chemistry; this mixed-up body merely housed the real person.

Far from the scene at the time, I depended on reports from friends to give me the picture. The following is how I imagine the dramatic events surrounding his suicide.

A man is driving down the highway in a truck. He looks forward to his destination a great deal, having plenty of the best fuel available and an excellent driving instructor in the front seat beside him. His truck, however, is overloaded with baggage. Having been on the road for a long time, he stops often to rebalance the awkward load. He looks around for assistance, but any assistance appears inadequate to him. Many of his fellow travelers are the very ones who had told him that God stills all storms. Somehow the other vehicles seem too far away, and at a glance their vehicles don't look any more roadworthy than his.

A rainstorm hits. Thunder, lightning, and then hailstones as big as ice cubes fall from the sky. Blinded, he can no longer see the center line on the well-marked road. The pounding of hail on the truck's roof becomes intolerable. The storm doesn't blow over, and his headlights only reveal more precipitation ahead. He loses visual perspective. The hail and thunder make it difficult to hear his companion's voice. Water begins to seep in around the doors. Where is the road? He is desperate. In the incredible weariness that washes over him, any exit, any halt becomes desirable.

Those who have not sinned may cast the first hailstone. Two or three melt in my hand.

Rev. Mac's baggage included his memories as a chaplain during the Korean war, of soldiers dying in pain—atrocities he had shared with only one friend that I know of. All his adult life he had awaited heaven with joy and enthusiasm, had been energized by truth, had traveled with God, but maybe his version of victory needed to be redefined to include the freedom to humanly hurt and still be found faithful.[3]

Our church sometimes insisted on a sort of victory that made for a quiet deceit in which we wore smiling masks, hiding pain that we thought might seem un-Christian. Trying to be more than human, we tarnished our transparency. We needed to find a new definition for Christian victory that bore no resemblance to Halloween, a pagan pretense, but we liked our masks. We found it hard to admit fear, anxiety, or struggle, preferring emotional hide-and-seek . . . or hide-and-please-don't-seek, because we wanted to appear spiritual and superhuman. We needed to accept the reality that God does not always enact miracles that still every storm and heal every ill.

One unanswerable question stimulates compassion: For *this* man to commit suicide, how great must the terror have been? May I never know that terror!

None of us can flesh out what terror or suffering means for another person because pain is individual and indefinable. What is pain to me may not be pain to you. Some people have high thresholds for pain—unidentified barriers against pain's assault—and handle physical pain differently than others who do not have high pain thresholds. Inevitable weakness and the prospect of falling apart blurred Rev. Mac's perspective. He was worn out. He made a frightful choice, but for him at that crucial time, when motive, means, and opportunity met, a quick exit seemed acceptable.

I will never know what made the pastor's last straw become the last straw, but I know this: God offered him tender care in illness but left him the choice of accepting his gentle mercies or rejecting them. God would not override Rev. Mac's free choice. When Rev. Mac first thought of suicide, God did not rush in with a panicked secondary plan to spare himself some embarrassment.

Karen has thought often of suicide but refuses it. She wants to know God truly, not as life superficially presents him. Pastor Mac's widow, Arlene, wants to know God as he truly is, not as her husband's death seems to present him.

Thank God, even with limitations on our understanding of Rev. Mac's choice, even with the spiritual vertigo of the moment, we need not faint. We are renewed in strength day by day, and even the questions that seem devastating stem from the troubles that achieve for us "an eternal glory that far outweighs them all" (2 Cor. 4:16–17).

I cannot imagine the startled wonder that Rev. Mac experienced upon entering God's glory. One second, black depression; the next, awe at God's glory and being in the arms of his heavenly Father. An unbroken hope fulfilled.

3

My Story

I felt as if I were going under, not to come up again. I wasn't experiencing terror like Rev. Mac's, but I thought, during a time of grief a few years ago, that I was going under. When I tried to sleep, I'd dream of drowning—successive dreams of drowning in oceans, lakes, or rivers. Oddly enough, considering my nightmares, friends who didn't know about them decided to help me recover by taking me canoeing!

I heard the soft splash of paddles as I sat huddled in the center of the canoe. Two friends were doing the work as we crossed the lake at dusk, and like all else, the action seemed far away. Many of you know grief; it is like that. Those who have grieved far more than I often describe the distance they sense as being several steps removed from what goes on around them.

Yes, I continued going to work. Apparently I functioned well enough and carried on routines like grocery shopping, as well as the greater demands of relating to others, but the distance was there. It was as if I had developed a permanent wince and had to concentrate in order to keep a normal facial expression. It was as if my responses were numbed, and yet every emotion pressed deeper than usual. My wish for the welcome escape of sound sleep was blocked by insomnia and then by the nightmares.

No person dear to me had died, but a set of treasured relationships had. Or at least they had suffered life-threatening wounds, and though I had never seen myself as qualified to be a martyr, I began to wonder about candidacy! To understand something of the level of my loss, you need to know me better.

I remained single while I was in nursing school and college, while working for a few years in the U.S., during nine years in Africa, and throughout the subsequent years in seminary. The responsibilities, opportunities, and privileges of these years are strongly positive. I enjoyed life, but as a relational person, described by others as warm and outgoing, the inevitable lonely times were difficult.

Only single, childless, affectionate women will understand with empathy what my life has been like: There is the exaggerated sense of not having been chosen by any man in the world, along with the knowledge that the possibility of motherhood is becoming more and more remote. There is the frustration of countless roommates or housemates who always seem to move just when shared furniture, at long last, seems to match. Such moves begin as an inconvenience in one's twenties, but after fifteen housemates, become a drain on self-esteem. There is the task of walking a tightrope of intimate relationships, choosing nonsexual closeness to match the holiness of a Christian lifestyle. There are the verbal and nonverbal suggestions by some married folks that single people are somehow less than adult—they haven't succeeded yet, or they are some kind of threat, and less than Christian if they admit to unfulfilled desires.

I found, though, that my making solid, pure, and caring friendships relieved most of the distress of heading toward middle age without husband or children. Four or five significant single friends, an older couple, and a family of five made me feel an important part of their lives. I could thrive as long as they included me. I doubt I could have managed well without them; I understood God's love at a feeling level because they generously displayed it to me. I needed them, and I thought they needed me.

Then, out of the blue, the family made plans to relocate several hundred miles away, announcing it to me as if I were a disinterested acquaintance in whom no emotional response was appropriate. Even explaining how I felt seemed unacceptable. I was not a part of the family as I had mistakenly thought and as I had quietly feared. Their decision was made immediately before we took a ten-day jaunt together, but they told me just after we arrived back home. So the memories of that vacation lost their shine, tarnished by deceit, or so it felt to me. I felt rejected. I grieved for what I had lost.

The awful grimness of that pain, the dear faithfulness of other friends, and the reality of a beautiful, solid hope that God gave me are the vivid memories that form the backdrop for what I have to say in these pages.

In those months I often reread the writings of Amy Carmichael and was encouraged to find that another single, childless, affectionate woman had already recorded on paper what I felt. She and I were famished forests and parched pools; burning winds had blown away soft blue mists, and brought too much solitude, songlessness, and silence.[1] Solitude is wonderful to me for restoring energy if loved ones are somewhere on the horizon, but solitude quickly became loneliness when these five folks moved out of my life.

The "parched-pool poem" concludes, "Where Thou art, all is well." I held onto the fact of God's presence and grasped a brief line that I had learned from the housemother for the nurses I had taught in Africa. "God knows," she had said when I had pneumonia and wanted to return to the classroom before I was well. Over and over she said, "God knows."

God knew the family was leaving. God was there, very "there." But they left, giving no opportunity for closure and healing. I hurt so much. I could not say all was well, but something was well. I cried for many hours, for days, and yet some way-deep-down corner was being comforted by God. The combination was strange.

Not long after, I began my academic study of Romans 5, a study of Paul's incredible statement about suffering and hope. Having been devastated, the only enduring help to be found was this truth. Even so, it took years for me to deeply apply the truth that Paul wrote.

Was *my* suffering covered by Paul when he said that suffering produced hope, or was he just talking about saints in long-ago centuries and missionaries trying to penetrate foreign cultures? He also wrote, "rejoice in suffering," but was he writing about pain that hurt this much? And could I, of all things, "rejoice"? Over the next few years, after the family's move, the academic study of these truths became personal. Theory became practice. Truth that I, at first, mentally understood developed at a felt, experienced level, so that it seemed like brand-new truth.

Even at the start, I had in mind what Paul meant. I could have defined his terms just as he defined them. You can probably think of times when you were talking with someone, and suddenly realized that your words and his didn't have the same meaning. A student once said to me that she had "flagged" an exam. Was I to be glad or to sympathize? I finally found out that she meant she had failed, while my first interpretation had been that she had come through with flags flying! If I could not understand what a fellow student meant, speaking my language in my century, how much more did I need to check Paul's definitions.

I had to reflect on what Paul meant by the words *suffering, hope, patience, character,* and *glory*. And when he ex-

panded on Romans 5:3–4 in Romans 8:17–30, what did he
mean by *frustration*? What could he possibly have meant in
chapter 8 when he wrote that creation was subjected to frustration in *hope*? I needed a theology for frustration!

This is what I found: *My pain did create hope.* After the
heavy emotions, the brooding, and the hard thinking, I chose
to own God's truth, and my black-and-blue pain produced
polished, golden twenty-four-karat hope.

Can you believe it? Suffering, *your* suffering, whatever its
specifics, however deep the hurt, can actually create in you
a very solid hope that connects inextricably with glory. Pain
is able to produce a wealth of firm hope for brilliant, unimaginable glory. Your particular suffering can widen and deepen
your knowledge of God. Suffering can increase not only your
knowledge about him, but the priceless joy of knowing him
well, of participating in his glory. But . . . you will still hurt,
maybe for a long while.

> Our tribulation, without ceasing to be tribulation or to be
> felt as tribulation, is transformed. . . . Our suffering is no
> longer a passive, dangerous, poisonous, destructive tribula-
> tion and perplexity . . . but is . . . creative, fruitful, power-
> ful, promising.[2]

When you think of your chief area of struggle, don't you
see it as passive, dangerous, poisonous, destructive, or per-
plexing, just as I saw my hurt in the wounded friendship?
Can you imagine that your trials could produce something
creative, fruitful, powerful, and promising? Yes, it would be
a gradual process, and it would require the difficult task of
working through deep emotions, but can you picture it? Can
you picture your suffering as the raw material of glory? Perhaps it is very raw material, but placed in the hands of the
ultimate Creator "in *this* situation, *as it is*, he is so mightily
God."[3]

Is this *your* situation? Remember my illustrations of Karen's multiple sclerosis and Steve's multiple abuses? And yes, remember Rev. Mac who catapulted into the full realization of heaven's glory? Through Romans learn with me from their lives *and* Rev. Mac's death. Allow what Rev. Mac, in his terror of the end, could not accept: the potential of personal suffering to be creative, fruitful, powerful, and promising.

Henri Nouwen tells the story of a man in mid-life who was diagnosed as having a fatal leukemia. Everything changed. Gradually, however, his questions changed from "Why me?" and "Why do I deserve this?" to "What is the promise hidden in this event?"[4] In his pain, he found a hidden promise.

How can pain be a positive part of life? To explain how this happened in my life I lightheartedly offer you this advice. Hang a little sign on your telephone. "CAUTION: Do *not* touch in the event of intermittent ringing." I suggest this because I dared to answer the phone a few years ago, not realizing how it would change my life. The long-term result was my moving twelve hundred miles away from several significant friends. You can imagine how stressful this was! I also had to resign from a job that I had hoped to hold until early retirement at age ninety-five. I walked away from opportunities as fulfilling as any I had known.

Of course, there were also all the little hassles of getting papers for the dog to cross the U.S.-Canadian border, being certain that my bills were paid and mail was forwarded, changing license plates from Saskatchewan to Illinois, and having immigration write me off their books as abandoning Canada.

But, back to that amazing phone call. Minutes after I had said a routine, "Hello," the gentleman on the other end asked if I was planning my usual vacation visit to the U.S. He had been wondering if we might explore a friendship and consider marriage. Just like that! After only a forty-five minute preamble! It is perhaps time to tell you that he and I were not strangers. We had worked in the same office a few years before, so he had not picked my phone number at random. We knew that we respected each other. His wife had passed away quite suddenly months before, leaving him and his seventeen-year-old daughter, Rebecca. They had been an unusually close family, and I had been praying for the right woman for him—one who would be a friend for Rebecca. I had no idea that I was praying about myself.

I left everything behind—retaining my Canadian friendships—that I might know and be known by Jim and his daughter, who by then was my good friend. To tell the truth, I recommend answering phones, because Jim and Rebecca are worth the hassle. They are much more than worth the hassle. Quite simply put, it is my privilege to know them.

The years between the loss of the family mentioned earlier and Jim's first call had been a time of spiritual growth for me. I had moved out of Psalm 4:6, "Who can show us any good?" I had entered Psalm 4:7, "You have filled my heart with greater joy than when their grain and new wine abound." I had experienced quite a transfer from perpetually asking God for what I didn't have to being overwhelmed with what I already had in him.[5]

The switch occurred when Romans 5 finally hit home and settled in my soul. Paul writes that suffering creates patience, character, and hope. In fact, I experienced this more than once over the years while I was writing my master's thesis on this passage. A bit odd, I thought, that Paul could write about the fruit of suffering so confidently; that such an undesirable activity as suffering could produce something as desirable as hope.

But it happened to me. It happened in me.

I began to catch on. Paul considered everything in his past as nothing, for one all-surpassing privilege—that he might know Christ (Phil. 3:7–11). Knowing Christ meant a personal relationship in which Christ would influence him totally. It meant having a full comprehension of Christ that would deepen in the process of daily experience.

Paul's knowing Christ meant his reevaluating all values; a continual forgetting of what was behind him, an absolute refusal to let them hold his attention and prevent his progress. It meant intimacy and total identification with Christ. It meant that the power that had earlier brought about the resurrection was operating in all sorts of matters in his everyday life. It was power being applied constantly in his development.

Knowing Christ meant the inevitable consequence of suffering, but the pain would be endurable because of the energizing of resurrection power. For Paul and for me, the fellowship of his sufferings *follows* the power of the resurrection—the power is available first, and then the management of our struggles, not vice versa.[6]

And struggle I did when marriage was so suddenly an option because before Jim called I had begun to value my relationship with God above all else. I had begun to tap resurrection power for my personal life and my job. Now I was actually afraid that a romantic relationship and possibly a marriage would spoil my intimacy with God, which was becoming so sweet. Obedience had given way to joy *without* Jim. I was lonely sometimes, yes, but seldom, because God was quite noticeably there.

So, in answer to the question, was it truly a hassle to leave Canada and marry Jim? Yes. My maturing happiness and an even deeper joy made it hard to allow him into my life. Suffering had sharpened my view of God, and for a while Jim's caring was a questionable interruption. Was his proposal a temptation or an opportunity? Knowing that God is everything, I thought that my depending on a man might get in the way.

Of course, this struggle was not comparable to an unavoidable diagnosis or a disabling rejection as in Karen's and Steve's cases, but I tell you my story for three reasons.

First, I want everyone to know that God met me. He met my needs convincingly, prior to and apart from Jim. All else aside, knowing God meant everything to me.

Second, I want everyone to realize that God continues to meet me daily "in the empty nursery." Jim arrived too late to help me populate a playroom, unless of course, God were scheduling a sequel to Abraham and Sarah's lives. But my knowing God is everything; nothing else can compare.

And third, I want everyone to see that the hassle of details, the reluctance in giving up a life I had come to love, the real pain of leaving friends who were like family, all these were worth it, that I might know and be known by Jim.

Knowing Jim swept me up and carried me away. It can be the same with Christ. You and I may have excruciating pain and innumerable hurts. Nevertheless out of them, and even because of them, hope grows; amazingly, hope can take over.[7] The privilege and reality of knowing God sweep us up and carry us away. For me, my well-loved friends' rejection gave me a new and overwhelming sense of acceptance by God and a desire to know him far better. Like Karen we must determine to know God as he truly is—not as life superficially presents him.

4

Paul's Life at Thorn's Point

"My current sufferings aren't worth comparing with the glory that will be revealed in me" (Rom. 8:18, paraphrased). On hearing such a statement, you might say, "No, that's too much to accept." But this is from Paul, the author, writing under the influence of God. Paul is extremely well qualified to broach the sensitive subject of human suffering, having lived a good part of his life with a "thorn" in his flesh that he had prayed to have removed (2 Cor. 12:7–10). Despite his prayers, the thorn stayed right where it was!

Under the experience section of his "resume," Paul is able to claim having survived countless pressures and afflictions. The following is just a sample:

Acts 9
A three-day blindness; loss of control; being led by
    others,
A plot against him (his basket-escape),
Rejection; the disciples not believing or accepting
    him,
Attempts of certain Jews to murder him.

Acts 13
Opposition from a magician,
Contradiction and jealousy of the Jews,
Serious harassment and being driven from the city.

Acts 14
Bitterness; threats of mistreatment and stoning,
Escape,
Efforts of others to make him a "god,"
Stoning and being abandoned as dead.

Acts 15
Dissension over circumcision,
Sharp disagreement with Barnabas over Mark.

Acts 16
Confrontations;
    with the evil spirit in the slave girl,
    with her owners,
Physical abuse in public,
Imprisonment.

Acts 17
Threats; being smuggled by night to Berea,
Pursuit; from Thessalonica, to Athens by sea,
Inner turmoil over the idols in Athens.

Acts 18
Resistance by and blasphemy of the Jews in Corinth.

While in Ephesus, he endured the obstinacy and disobedience of his listeners, including those who "publicly maligned the Way" (Acts 19:9). Can you imagine how such talk would affect the mind and heart of Paul, so committed to "thy Way"? Can you imagine Paul's stress because the crowds demanded healing and exorcism? Can you imagine the confusion and danger that the silversmith created over profits and losses for shrine manufacturers? Yet, Paul managed to write at least two letters to the people of Corinth, letters that, *in the middle of* his struggles, express the concept of hope growing out of suffering. We are fairly certain that he wrote First and Second Corinthians from Ephesus as the events of Acts 19 transpired.[1] Nevertheless, even under those circumstances, he was able to focus his writing on the needs of the Corinthians, a focus he received from outside himself.

Paul was not preaching contentment. He wrote to the Corinthians as a toad beneath the sharp iron teeth and discs of a harrow. Paul knew the harrow well. He knew abrasions and wounds. He knew adrenaline pushing his pulse up. He knew perspiring palms, a dry mouth, fear, misunderstanding, anger, and indignation.[2] He also knew the "thorn in the flesh." After all, the apostle had nerve endings that carried pain messages, blood pressure that could skyrocket, knotted neck muscles after a long day's work, and blood that stained. He was just like us.

At this point Paul could already claim a history of hard work. He could also report imprisonment; flogging, stoning, and beatings with rods (and the resultant bruises and soreness); repeated exposures to death; thirty-nine lashings on five occasions; two shipwrecks (there was yet one to come); a night and day in the open sea; and constant travel with few amenities (2 Cor. 11:23–25).

Writing to the people at Corinth, he also lists dangers in rivers, at sea, in the city, and in the country, as well as peril at the hands of the Jews, the Gentiles, bandits, and false brothers. He experienced physical distress because of the lack of sleep, food, and water. His clothing was inadequate and the heat too great. He also felt the squeeze of great responsibility for churches still at the teething stage (2 Cor. 11:26–28). In spite of all of these hardships, Paul could still write, "I delight in weaknesses, in insults, in hardships, in persecutions, in difficulties" (2 Cor. 12:10).

Wouldn't you like to talk with Paul, and ask, "How could you say that and mean it? Precisely what *did* you mean? What I want to know, Paul, is how you arrived at wanting to know Christ *and* the fellowship of his sufferings. How did you discover the reality of being able to say, 'sorrowful, yet always rejoicing,' or 'in all our troubles, my joy knows no bounds'?" (2 Cor. 6:10; 7:4).

Paul was authentic. He wrote with integrity and sincerity, totally convinced of the truth. He was an apostle, but still a human being. Flesh-and-blood human, yet an unusual, exceptional person with an incredible assignment from God: to write truth.

Paul was unusual. He saw visions and was "caught up to the third heaven." He experienced the "sentence of death" and "despaired of life." He helped establish the thrust of missions, and wrote a large part of the New Testament. He firmly confronted colleagues, and yet wrote tenderly that he couldn't stand it when separated from his friends in Thessalonica. (I like him for that—both for feeling the separation and for telling them directly that he felt torn away from them and yearned to see them again.) He was gentle among them like a mother, as well as strongly encouraging among them like a father.[3]

My father used to label select people as "real." He never defined what he meant by it, but after meeting numerous "real" people, I could see that they were genuine and honest about themselves and their thoughts. They, according to my father's description, were people who, no matter how far they climbed, were always down-to-earth!

Paul was real because he was human like us, and because he was a person with a place in history. He was real according to my dad's definition because he was genuine, honest, and down-to-earth, even though he was an apostle. In the presence of pain, he integrated theology with life in a way that makes us want to rip open his letters in order to learn from him.

Paul was the follower of Another who was real—who was human, historic, genuine, honest, and down-to-earth in a magnificent way. He didn't aspire to be important—equality with God had been his from eternity. Rather, he humbled himself. The Lord Jesus Christ suffered beyond description (in fulfillment of Isaiah's "Suffering Servant" prophecy [Isa. 53]), and "was crowned with *glory* . . . because he *suffered* death" (Heb. 2:9; emphasis mine).

Paul wanted the all-surpassing privilege of knowing Christ, including the power of his resurrection and the fellowship of his sufferings. He wanted to be like Christ. This consciousness of himself as a servant of God, being transformed into Christ's likeness, may be the key to Paul's attitude toward affliction.[4] He introduced himself in his letters as a servant and gave us the servant hymn in Philippians 2.

Your attitude should be the same as that of Christ Jesus:
Who being in very nature God,
   did not consider equality with
     God something to be
     grasped,
but made himself nothing,
   taking the very nature of a servant,
   being made in human likeness.
And being found in appearance as a man,
   he humbled himself
   and became obedient to death—
     even death on a cross!

Therefore God exalted him to the
   highest place
and gave him the name that is
   above every name,
that at the name of Jesus every knee
   should bow,
   in heaven and on earth and under
   the earth,
and every tongue confess that Jesus
   Christ is Lord,
   to the glory of God the Father.
                  Philippians 2:5–11

God said to Ananias of Paul, "I will show him how much he must suffer for my name" (Acts 9:16). Paul told early disciples that they would "go through many hardships to enter the kingdom of God." Luke reports that these words were to give strength and courage to assist the disciples in remaining true to the faith (Acts 14:22). Suffering was no accident, no side issue, no surprise, no footnote. It was enough that a servant be like his master (Matt. 10:25).

Perhaps this explains how a person could go through all the conflict of Acts 19 (mentioned earlier), and still have positive energy left to *encourage* the disciples in Ephesus (Acts 20:1–3). Perhaps this explains why Paul, against such a stormy backdrop, could in the following three months write such a book as Romans, in which he teaches that suffering produces the hope of glory and is not worth comparing with the glory that is yet to come. Chaos, riots, danger, and travel . . . I would have insisted on a three-month vacation, and perhaps would have dropped a brief thank-you note to my recent hosts in Ephesus. Not Paul. He wrote Romans.

And throughout this man's letters, there is the constant pendulum-like swing from suffering to hope, suffering to glory, suffering to rejoicing, suffering to joy, suffering to delight. A metronome used by a musician can hardly be more regular than Paul's swings in connecting suffering to hope. It is as if the word *suffering* triggered hope, glory, and joy in his mind as predictably as the word *walk* triggers an excited frenzy in my collie-shepherd. On a decidedly grander level, suffering triggers hope—the hope of glory.

Of the Macedonian believers, Paul said, "Out of the most severe *trial*, their overflowing *joy* and their extreme poverty welled up in rich generosity." He asked the Ephesian people not to be discouraged, and said that his *sufferings* for them equated with their *glory*. To the Colossians he said, "I *rejoice* in what was *suffered* for you." This is more than a polite "Glad to do it for you," or " 'Tweren't nothin'." He recognized that "in spite of severe *suffering*," the Christians at Thessalonica "welcomed the message with . . . *joy*."⁵

Hope. Glory. Eager expectation. Glorious freedom. Joy. These are the "ticks" of suffering lived out through Christ. Suffering and hope. Ticktock. Suffering and glory. Ticktock. . . .

Be still. Be quite still. It may require silence to hear a ticktock. And what if we choose not to listen very, very carefully? We can expect to hear only the "ticks" or only the "tocks"—a weirdly broken rhythm.

Rhythms
in Romans

The gospel . . . is the power of God for the salvation of everyone who believes. . . . A righteousness from God is revealed, a righteousness that is by faith from first to last. . . . The righteous will live by faith.

Romans 1:16–17

Participation in suffering means to suffer with Christ, to encounter God, as Jeremiah and Job encountered Him; to see Him in the tempest, to apprehend Him as light in the darkness, to love Him when we are aware only of the roughness of His hand. . . . In the Spirit, suffering . . . can become our advance in the glory of God.

Karl Barth

The gospel is God's effective power active in the world of men to bring about . . . reinstatement in that glory of God which was lost through sin— that is, salvation [in the end] which reflects its splendour back into the present.

C. E. B. Cranfield

5

Facing the Facts

Abraham faced the fact of his total inadequacy, but was fully persuaded of God's power to fulfill his promises (Rom. 4:19–21). God taught Abraham to face earthly facts, to acknowledge his own deadness, but to *look at* the *unseen*. Talk about perspective! Like Abraham, we who believe stay in touch with the facts of life, but fix our eyes on the eternal, the invisible (2 Cor. 4:18).

Paul wrote of being "hard pressed on every side, but not crushed; perplexed, but not in despair" (2 Cor. 4:8). Such pressure and perplexity are facts of life. What element stands in the gap between the squeezing pressure and the cracking crunch, between bewilderment and an even worse bleakness? Isn't it hope? For Paul and for us to gain such a perspective of hope requires a "wrestling, a stretching out with every effort of the soul" to God, a search beyond the seen to the invisible.[1] A spiritually energetic stretching that, *once chosen and begun,* will inevitably be rewarded by finding God's hand, already extended toward us.

Inevitably? Yes, *if a person chooses* the Godward reach, as Abraham and Sarah did. Inevitably for Karen and Steve? Yes, through and beyond disease and abuse. Inevitably for Rev. Mac? Yes, God's hand was there through and beyond the dreadful shortcut of suicide. God reaches out to all of us, whatever our circumstances or condition. God continues to take the initiative, and his initiative is never hesitant, nor tentative. His accessibility is inevitable because of the historical event of the cross of Christ, and God's initiative taken at Calvary is a fact we must face. He longs for our response.

More appealing truths await us later in Romans, but we must first accept the groundwork that Paul lays. He reviews the dire need of people in sin, the horrid condition of wickedness and isolation from God. Each of us must face the fact of individual sinfulness and need. As difficult as it is and though we would like to determinedly avoid it, you and I must understand our brokenness before we can begin, by grace, to overcome it. Then we will be able to appreciate more fully the wholeness that is accessible through Christ. At the end of Romans 3 Paul carries us, if we will allow him, from despair to joy. Salvation and forgiveness trumpet in.

Salvation by faith, redemption from sin, hope after depression, glory beyond suffering—aren't these incredible possibilities? Paul reminds us that Abraham believed the unlikely, the facts behind the facts, the unbelievable, the impossible, because *God* promised it. He believed God

> who gives life to the dead and calls things that are not as though they were. Against all hope, Abraham in hope believed and so became the father of many nations, just as it had been said to him, "So shall your offspring be." Without weakening in his faith, he faced the fact that his body was as good as dead—since he was about a hundred years old—and that Sarah's womb was also dead. Yet he did not waver through

unbelief regarding the promise of God, but was strengthened in his faith and gave glory to God, being fully persuaded that God had power to do what he had promised.

Romans 4:17–21[2]

For us, it seems absolutely impossible that suffering can contain seed for the hope of glory. Was it any more possible that two confirmed geriatrics, Abraham and Sarah, could from their seed give birth to a baby? Abraham lived his role in salvation history as an ancestor of Jesus Christ and faced the fact of two matched but obsolete reproductive systems, yet he still believed God's power was operative—the fact behind the fact.

You and I must face directly the fact of our total inability to generate hope and to rejoice in God. Doesn't God have the power to do what he has promised in Romans 5, the power to do what seems altogether unlikely? Doesn't God by his Spirit have the power to bring hope out of suffering, as we walk by faith?

While we are handling the unlikely, try thinking of suffering as *therapy*. Paul shows us that suffering acts as therapy to return us to glory. Face the fact: We need spiritual therapy to find our way from sin to glory. "For all have sinned and fall short of the glory of God" (Rom. 3:23). This verse carries us back to the Garden of Eden where man and woman first sinned and forfeited God's intended glory. God had told Adam and Eve that they were free to eat of any tree in the garden, but he said, "You must not eat from the tree of the knowledge of good and evil, for when you eat of it you will surely die" (Gen. 2:17). They ate of this tree in the middle of a green garden that was lush with desirable, permissible fruit. Adam and Eve died spiritually and thus lost their previous enjoyment of God and his glory. They tried to become gods themselves, rather than responding to the true God in appropriate obedience. They chose for themselves a path of death that included the knowledge and experience of evil, with all the suffering that extends from death and evil. They chose just as you and I would have.

But this path of suffering turned out to be the route back to glory. Paul tells us that creation was subjected by God to a form of suffering, suffering called frustration, and that God subjected creation in *hope* that it would be liberated into *glorious* freedom. Repeatedly, Paul makes the point that suffering creates the hope of glory for the believer (Rom. 3:23; 8:20; 5:3–4; 2 Cor. 4:16–18).

God's end for us and for all creation is glory. Suffering is a means to that end. What did it mean for Adam and Eve that suffering was an alternate route to glory? It meant that many kinds of pain were necessary to remind them of their limitations and inadequacies, because only when clearly reminded would they realize that they were not gods. And only when reminded repeatedly would they learn to become obedient to the true God.

Adam and Eve did not comprehend the truth any faster than you and I do. A lifetime was required for them to understand deeply and truly that they were not gods, but that God was God. One or two minor scrapes were not sufficient, but full-blown suffering became necessary.

Such therapy seems unnecessarily rigorous until I remember that I am Eve's equivalent. I must acknowledge my inability to grasp that I am not God. I must confess my frequent attempts to take complete control of my universe for my own glory; however, when I am somehow hurt, I recall that I am a limited and flawed human being who desperately needs an infinite and perfect God. Then, at last, rather weary from failing efforts to rule my self and my scene, I kneel to say, "My father in heaven, may your name be glorified. Your kingdom come. Your will be done . . . for the power and glory must be yours" (portions of Matt. 6:9–13, paraphrased).

Adam and Eve were disciplined, but they received something far better than a paternal spanking. The discipline was therapy. Suffering became therapy, and suffering formed the route back to glory. Knowing that his glory is our highest good, God chose the best map to reroute us to glory, a map that was not his preference. The route leads through valleys of death and pain, but the map leads as well over hope-filled gaps.

This is hard to swallow because we want ease. C. S. Lewis writes that

> we are half-hearted creatures, fooling about with drink and sex and ambition when infinite joy is offered us, like an ignorant child who wants to go on making mud pies in a slum because he cannot imagine what is meant by a holiday at the sea. We are far too easily pleased.[3]

6

Forgiven and Accepted

"One thing I have done all my life, I have tried to please God." Not such an amazing sentence, until you learn that it was spoken by my father, who was well advanced into Alzheimer's disease when he managed to string together these fourteen sensibly combined words. Even in Alzheimer's, Dad would have agreed with an accident survivor who once said, "*Life* is unfair, God is *not*."[1] Dad had seen beyond the visible, had found God awaiting his reach. Like Abraham, Dad knew his own limitations and banked on God's power. He knew his own sinfulness and God's readiness to step in and provide wholeness. Dad saw through physical reality to spiritual reality.

Dad knew spiritual reality, spiritual life, at a deep level, though the vocabulary of Romans, words like *justification* and *reconciliation,* would have sent him to his reference books. But knowing he was forgiven and accepted, he enjoyed the truth beyond the theological terms. He knew the rhythm of Paul's music.

In the world of music, a concerto employs one or more solo instruments playing with an orchestra. Romans, to me, is a concerto for organ and trumpet. Not just any organ will suffice. This is a pipe organ—no substitutes allowed because to describe Romans we must have the best! Not just any organist will do either, but a well-taught, well-practiced one, since the purposeful movement and controlled energy of the musician pictures for us the powerful activity of God's recapturing his world. Thus, the organ sounds the dignity of men and women declared righteous by God.

Now listen. As an echo to the organ, you will hear the trumpet with its theme: justification. Justification goes beyond God's fairness: It is a trumpet call, brilliant, beautiful, shining, crisp, clear, full of joy, and announcing forgiveness.

What is justification? Justification is better defined in a courthouse than in a concert hall, but Paul places us in the only courtroom where lovely music belongs. The accused comes before the judge. Those guilty as charged are you or I, or Karen, or Steve, or Rev. Mac. The judge is God. Then, into this courtroom comes the Advocate, Jesus Christ, who not only has power to present the case, but enters the witness stand with, and for, each of us. The righteousness of Christ is bestowed on us who are correctly charged, guilty of sin. God's pronouncement: "I find the defendant not guilty." We are acquitted—a joyful, sweet word in the ears of the accused—paid in full by Christ as an expression of God's faithfulness. Justification is forgiveness by God, the judge. It is a forgiveness because of an individual's faith in Christ.[2]

Not content with a picture from the courtroom, Paul moves to the social sphere, discussing reconciliation. There is no relationship between the judge and the accused in the imagery of justification, but in reconciliation there is true self-engagement on the part of God toward the sinner.[3] This is music to our ears: God forgives us, and hallelujah, the God of the universe allows himself to be known by us. We are accepted.

Reconciliation is an emotionally charged term that expresses the change of status and feeling in the relationship between God and us. There we are! Believers, justified in the courtroom, formerly enemies, then reconciled so that we become God's intimates! We are transformed in God's presence. Jesus Christ stands at the pivotal point between our being sinners fearing wrath, and our being justified persons awaiting glory; between me, June Terry, unreconciled and God's enemy, and June Terry, reconciled and accepted as God's intimate.

Jesus Christ *is* the pivot from the old to the new, from death to resurrection life, from despair to joy, from suffering to glory. God delights in such deliverances, and as believers we find ourselves transferred from the old aeon, the dominion of death, into the new aeon, the age of Christ. This new aeon does not have so much to do with the era of time we are living in, as with a change in the nature of life. Life incredibly reigns over death, and hope grows out of suffering.

Not that the old aeon has vanished. Ask any hurting person! Or, if you are a Christian currently experiencing pain or with a clear memory of distress, you needn't ask anyone. Temptation, trial, and pressure remain, but God has burst in on the scene with the dominion of life, calling us to enter it with him. Life in Christ is of a totally different quality, and puts even deep hurt into an entirely new light.

The blessings that we *already* have in life with God are innumerable, but there are indescribable blessings that we have *not yet* seen or heard—so many that we would be knocked over by the full knowledge if they were known. While we live in the "already" of developing hope, we also live in the "not yet," because human suffering is still present. We begin to see all of life from a new perspective, and with this new perspective, we start to see beyond suffering to its results. We learn to share the fellowship of his sufferings while depending on the power of his resurrection. We can eventually place a positive value on suffering. We penetrate reality. We almost see through it.[4]

My father is a case study of an ordinary man with a spiritual grasp on reality, and not just the reality found on the surface of life on the peninsula of Maryland where he spent his seventy-nine years. He had a hold on the ultimate reality. He could not have explained it this way, but he knew God was fair, yet he didn't expect life to be! He would have confessed to being imperfect, a sinner bathed in grace. He was one of those people with a shining face who seemed perpetually to have just learned a fun secret. But the source of his joy was no secret; he knew he was forgiven and accepted. He knew God.

Reconciled to God, and justified, my father had peace. He lived in the power of the resurrection, and in spite of suffering saw through the pain to live out and demonstrate God's hope. His early memories included the loss of his mother, and to his young mind, a stepmother who was difficult to accept. In his teens Dad went to work for the Coca-Cola Company, leaving home at six each morning for over forty years to walk to work. By the beginning of World War II, he had a wife and two children. After his service in Europe, he came home, wanting to repress the events he had witnessed. For a long time, he could not enjoy war movies on our little black-and-white television.

In 1963, seven tons of machinery fell on him at the Coke plant; he was nearly crushed, but for another piece of equipment that supported some of the weight and saved his life. He was critically ill for days, with internal injuries and numerous fractures. I flew home not expecting him to make it. There were many special prayer meetings for him. He made it! A hospital bed was moved into our home, and Mother cared for him for months after he was finally discharged from the hospital.

Following the accident, he retired early, and invested nearly twenty years in telling others of God's power, which had returned him to health much to the surprise of his doctors. He spoke wherever people welcomed him: in churches, prisons, hospitals, on beaches, and one-on-one in homes and at shopping malls. He gave away literally thousands of Gideon Bibles.

In the mid-1970s, he watched my mother die—edging downhill over a five-year span—yet he kept on reporting God's faithfulness and demonstrating it in his lifestyle. Later he remarried and shared everything he could about God with his new wife, Rachel. They had a delightful marriage.

Over the years I scrutinized my father's life, and I saw hope emerge, faith solidify, spiritual excitement dominate. I heard him cry to God for help and adore him out loud in the same sentence. Anyone who would listen learned about Scripture from him, and those who wouldn't, could not deny that Dad's nature reminded them of God. "Irrepressible" was not in his vocabulary, but irrepressibility gave his spirit a sort of carbonated fizz. But in 1984, the symptoms of Alzheimer's sneaked in, pouncing hard in 1985, pinning his shoulders to the mat by 1987.

During a period of pathetic befuddlement, he clearly declared his life's aim: to please God. The striking words came one day when Dad and Rachel went with Jim and me to Chincoteague Island, Virginia, one of Dad's favorite places. As we visited with my aunt, he inserted meaningless phrases, and by early afternoon was worried about staying away from home after dark. Then suddenly, he leaned toward us and with intensity pronounced that bold statement: "One thing I have done all my life, I have tried to please God!" This was his only rational sentence that day, except when we had asked if he wanted to thank God for the food, and he prayed coherently, feelingly.

The last time I saw him alive was seven months before his death. He was extremely anxious and fretful. No longer recognizing me, he was surprised that I would call him "Daddy."

That Sunday morning I sat with him in the nursing home lounge while some folks prepared for a small church service. He was tied to his chair, and I, to my grief. As soon as the pianist began to play old hymns, he broke into a broad smile, saying, "Oh, I'm okay now. I'm okay now." Calmed by the music, Dad began to sing the hymns, words in perfect order, note following correct note.

This was a poignant example of the "already" of a believer's hope, a solid hope though "not yet" fully experienced because of human limitations and suffering. Dad's was a determined, redeemed spirit, caught in the boundaries of a mortal body and a diseased mind. For months Dad was mentally out of touch with us. Early on the morning of December 28, 1988, Dad hurtled into God's lap with enthusiasm, set totally free from the old aeon. I guess if he had not been speechless at the glory, he would've asked those who welcomed him in heaven if they needed Gideon testaments. There were no more "not yets." He had arrived.

And I was left. As Jim says, "It is lousy to be the one left behind." Left behind with my own sorrow at losing Dad, my own series of "not yets," my own set of wearinesses, and maybe someday my own Alzheimer's.

Jim flew east with me for the funeral. The night before the service we went to the funeral home, which was a well-kept Victorian house. At least twenty-five black windows stared blankly at us when we arrived, like people not knowing what to say, but in each was a lighted Christmas candle whispering, "Yes, you feel Good-Friday bleak, but Christ has come and lighted the way to resurrection day."

On the steps was the December 30th newspaper, and I remember being surprised that newspapers were still being printed now that my Dad was dead. Flags should have been at half-mast; banks and businesses closed. I wondered how I would respond to giddy New Year's wishes.

Jim and I went in with Rachel, my stepmother, and there was my father's body. I didn't touch it, not wanting to know how dead it was. My dad was like a righteous David slain by a hateful Goliath, with the jagged stones of disease. But I knew the truth, reality that is grand in contrast to the temporal facts. He had taught me the real story, and I knew that he lived in God's presence, that death will die because of Christ, and that no matter how carefully or tightly that Maryland soil was packed the next day, Dad will, in the end, rise with others from all over the world who have died in Christ. And then . . . Dad will be glorified. No more sickening disintegration. He will wear a perfectly integrated body.

He has left me behind for now. But I was left with a heritage: life defeated death, heaven conquered Alzheimer's, despair seeded with joy, the hope of glory outstripped pain. He showed me that the Holy Spirit does not let go when Satan uses Alzheimer's to pummel God's child. He lived acquitted in God's court, forgiven, justified in Christ. Dad taught me very well of Jesus Christ—the sinner's only agent of reconciliation and my sure pivot of perspective.

7

From Faith to Faith

"Faith like Job's cannot be shaken because it is the result of *having been* shaken"[1] (italics mine). The tested faith of a veteran believer like my father differs from the faith of a new Christian. In Romans, Paul embraces both kinds of faith, both levels of development, both the young and mature believers. Philip Yancey calls the tested faith of the veteran, "fidelity, a deeper, more mysterious kind of faith." This is fidelity like Job's, "faith in its starkest form."[2]

But it would be premature to press fidelity on a Christian, young in faith, new to the Gospel, and caught deeply in pain. To him or her it would sound like badly timed optimism. I think especially of a man named Bill who cannot be offered any more than he can handle. To process verse upon verse, truth upon overexplained truth, would be too much for Bill right now.

Bill is caught on the suffering side of life, and he has not known Christ long. He will eventually find long-term faithfulness beyond his days of infant faith. But at twenty-one he is only three months past tragic injury—the loss of an arm and the loss of sight. His friends practice sitting with their eyes closed, trying to comprehend the loss of shape, color, shadow, and light. How long will he recall with accuracy just how "turquoise" turquoise can be? How long will Bill be able to "see" the faces of family, the femininity of women, the mechanisms of an engine? How long will he be able to remember pitching a baseball, or the excitement of seeing a quarterback deliver the football to a hole in the air exactly where his teammate reaches for it? Bill no longer sees or plays ball.

As Bill rode his motorcycle on a six-lane highway, he passed a car and re-entered an inside lane just as a pickup truck moved into the same lane. He was tragically injured. Now in a rehabilitation center, he does the hard work of processing his anger and the grief of the physical loss.

But his Christian friends have something to offer him— eventually. When the time is right, they will offer more of righteousness and power, more of faith and fidelity and grace, and much later, more about the way that suffering contributes to glory.

But when? Next year? The year after that? We hope someday he will be ready to hear about delight and joy in the glory of God and about how suffering fits in the life of faith. Young faith and veteran fidelity will someday combine so that Bill will hear the full rhythm and the music that God has composed.

To hear only the ticktock of rhythm without the variety of instruments, the changes of pitch, the texture of tones, the crescendos, the quiet places, and the overall beauty, would be a loss for the listener. Who wants to concentrate on only a ticktock without any music? Thus, we must listen to the entirety of Romans, one of the most important theological books ever written.

Nothing given by God in our lives is out of line with his salvation purpose, just as nothing in Romans is out of line with Paul's purposes for writing it (Rom. 1:8–13). Longing to visit the church in Rome, which he had not yet done, he wrote Romans to introduce himself and his beliefs, without which he hardly had an identity. He was too integrated to present either himself or his beliefs divorced from one another. In modern vernacular we would say, "Paul had it together."

He wrote as well to meet the needs of the mixed congregation in Rome where two groups of Christians were failing to mesh, the Gentiles and the Jews.[3] To establish the urgency and appropriateness of unity, he pointed to the bottom line—both Jews and Gentiles were sinners and both needed to be justified by faith. The Jews bragged about the law; the Gentiles enjoyed boasting about being grafted in as branches on God's family tree (Rom. 2:17–24; 11:17–21). Paul wrote to say that the "boasting" or rejoicing of the Christian must be above all in God himself through Christ and in the hope of glory. Then Paul faces the possible objection to rejoicing, even when we hurt. In suffering, which by God's Spirit conceives within us the seed of the hope of glory (Rom. 5:2, 3, 11; 2 Cor. 4:16–18).

Suffering causes faith to develop into fidelity. Suffering has its place as a part of the whole gospel, the gospel that dominates like a strong melody line in Romans.

> I am not ashamed of the gospel, because it is the power of God for the salvation of everyone who believes: first for the Jew, then for the Gentile. For in the gospel a righteousness from God is revealed, a righteousness that is by faith from first to last, just as it is written: "The righteous will live by faith."
>
> Romans 1:16–17

The gospel is not about power; the gospel *is* power. And in the gospel is righteousness from God, dynamically revealed not only for sinful men and women to observe from a wistful, unhappy distance but also for ownership, for personal participation—for Bill's participation, for yours and mine.

Distance dissolves. When I lived in South Africa, I once went to peek inside the doors of the Capetown hospital where the first heart transplant had been done. I expected to see only the outside of the building or at most, the reception area. To my surprise, a security guard introduced me to the director of nurses who proceeded to take me to see the operating suite where the surgery had been performed. I felt like a little girl who had pushed her nose against windows for a good look-see, only to have a hidden door swing open so that she fell inside.

So it is with the righteousness of God as it is revealed and given to people of faith. It is not as if we are just invited to stand outside with our noses pressed against the glass or allowed to touch hesitantly the fringe of his righteousness. We are welcomed in, taken on tour, and presented with the gift of his righteousness. Barriers dissolve and we actually get to know God. We become the willing slaves of righteousness rather than slaves of sin: "This righteousness from God comes through faith in Jesus Christ to all who believe" (Rom. 3:22).

One writer speaks of the righteousness of God being his power reaching out to the world, and of the world's salvation coming by being "recaptured for the sovereignty of God."[4] Thus recaptured, we will actually take part someday in the glory of God. Even now we can possess the solid hope of such participation. Do you begin now to hear the grandeur of Paul's concerto? Do you hear the gospel as a bright, singable melody with full harmony? Faith opens our ears to such music.

We are justified by faith, altogether by faith. Those made righteous by faith in Christ will live now and forever. Having come to him by faith, we continue to walk by faith throughout the rest of life. In the process, the initial faith and hope of the new Christian, the recruit, gradually become the tested faith and hope of the veteran.[5] And doesn't the faith of the trusting Christian seem most exercised in the arena of suffering?

For new Christians, unlike Bill, who have not yet suffered in their faith, we must avoid what Packer calls a cruel ministry carried out in "irresponsible kindness" where we teach people to expect a carefree existence once they belong to Christ. J. I. Packer writes that God leads his children from the

> glow of spiritual babyhood, with its huge chuckles and contented passivity, precisely in order that He may lead them into an experience . . . more adult and mature.[6]

Suffering hurts intensely. If we were to forget that, and overemphasize the hope of Romans, we could encourage a "childish, grinning . . . self-absorbed breed" of Christian adults.[7] Then, were they to suffer, they could become morbidly introspective, trying to figure out what they had done wrong to earn such treatment from God.

Patty, a young recruit to Christian faith en route to becoming a veteran, learned quickly about struggle. She had known Christ for a few years when I met her, and her faith and hope had begun to grow. Each year of spiritual exercise gave her more stability and strength. Though she was committed to the lifelong process of getting to know God fully, she was seduced into a friendship with a homosexual.

She learned quickly that the Christian life was not a carefree existence, that she could not be passive, that what she really wanted was a mature Christian lifestyle. Patty decided to come away from that relationship into healthier patterns, encouraged by God "perfect in power, in love, and purity."[8] She felt that withdrawing from the friendship was necessary, though the exit still meant loss. She was not ecstatic or gleeful by any stretch of the imagination. During our talks I watched her mature as she thought her way into under-standing, peace, wholesomeness, balance, consistency, quiet-ness, freedom, confidence, and yes, fidelity. Patty has ears to hear the music of Romans.

8

The Cross at the Center

"In me you may have peace." Nothing, no problem imaginable, can separate the Christian from God's love. Musa, an African nurse, put this into her own words. In the days when a perky starched cap served as a reward given early in one's nursing education, we withheld Musa's cap because of low grades and her need to improve in nursing skills. She said to her friends, "I will not allow a piece of starched cloth to come between me and God! I just won't." She forged ahead, learned well, and earned her cap. By her own choice, she would allow nothing to separate her from the enjoyment of God's love.

Romans assures us that God will allow nothing to separate us from his love. Although Christ's suffering was unique, Christians suffer in fellowship with him in a solidarity that cannot be fractured. Our troubles, correctly handled, enrich our knowledge of him and nudge us toward him at the feeling level, fostering a sense of healthy fusion with him.

This permanent bond with his love, this bond with him, is so fully forged, so intact, that we cannot comprehend it. He understood this fusion when he spoke with the disciples so that they might have peace, and then said, "In this world, you will have trouble. But take heart! I have overcome the world" (John 16:33). I have overcome the world; you will be more than conquerors!

We have come upon an important fact here in John's Gospel, "You will have trouble." Hidden in the very core of suffering is a *"must."*[1] There is no other way to live the Christian life. There was no other way for Christ; there is no other way for those who follow him. We are not delivered *from* suffering, but *for* suffering. These are hard words to accept, but God was direct with Paul about the necessity of suffering: "I will show him (Paul) how many things he *must* suffer for my name" (Acts 9:16; italics mine). Paul passed this message on to the disciples in Lystra, Iconium, Antioch, and Thessalonica. Peter left the same legacy in his writing. And from the writer to the Hebrews:

> But we see Jesus, who was made a little lower than the angels, now crowned with glory and honor, because he suffered death, so that by the grace of God he might taste death for everyone. In bringing many sons to glory, *it was fitting* that God, for whom and through whom everything exists, should make the author of their salvation perfect through suffering.
>
> Hebrews 2:9–10 (italics mine)

"It was fitting." Three difficult words to explain. And here, I believe, we are again back at the Garden of Eden, where the inevitability of suffering is first viewed. Back again to the point that when man and woman sinned, they forfeited glory, and the only return route led through terrain marked with suffering, suffering that was uncomfortable therapy. But thank God there was a way back through the indescribable suffering of the author of our salvation, so that suffering for us is but "for a little while" (1 Peter 1:6).

We are not locked into the "must" of suffering without Christ who has gone before us. We suffer in solidarity with and for him. John Stott writes that the cross cancels the "apparent God-forsakenness" of pain. "The Cross smashes to smithereens (the) terrible caricature of God," as an indifferent god, dozing in a celestial deck chair. Stott asks, "In the real world of pain, how could one worship a God who was immune to it?" He quotes Bonhoeffer, who writing from prison nine months before his execution, said, "Only the Suffering God can help."[2]

A few years ago astronauts recovered an "L-DEF," a "Long Duration Exposure Facility" with over fifty experiments aboard, left in space five years past the due date because of a disaster in the initial recovery plan. Early observations showed jagged rips in the outer surface and gouges from its rubbing "shoulders" with bits of space debris. Scientists and students investigated its cargo of seeds and eggs to learn the effects of lengthy "space shock" on them.

You and I are not mechanical L-DEF's abandoned in orbit in order to record the results of exposure to the elements. We are not cold, unfeeling, soulless metal objects requiring rescue by a god of limited power who sent us where he could not go, nor are we celestial experiments to be examined for emotional stress marks and spiritual potholes by a mad scientist of a god.

Rather, we worship a God who understands suffering, who knows hurt, who can help, and who is infinitely concerned. We are not left alone with a frosty definition of what we know already by experience: pressure and pain. We are not arrested in the stage of suffering, to remain there unrelieved or without God's understanding. We are moved ahead consistently toward the positive development of hope and joy and an expectation of glory. We know, and are getting to know better, a God who has suffered. A God who was not only there at Calvary, but was the central figure. The Prince of glory died, and in his dying fractured death; the Prince of glory is risen and lives.

Such is the courage and the wisdom of God's love, that with the high value of glory in view, he breaks through our barriers to give us the vision of an unimaginable panorama. It is this courageous, discerning love that the characters discuss in *The Other Side of the Sun*, by Madeleine L'Engle. In their battle between good and evil, they go through "the terrible light of the sun" and come out in joy. "Love has to go through darkness and pain and endurance and a stark acceptance before it can come out into the far light of the sun."[3] L'Engle's character, Miss Olivia, says,

> How did they bear it all? Mado lost her husband, four of her five children, . . . and her firstborn was drowned. When I look back on her life, it was one tragedy after another, and yet she was the most joyful person I have ever known. Mado had . . . scars of the soul . . . [She] was never bitter nor resentful.

Honoria doesn't allow Miss Olivia to keep her blind spot:

> Never? Miss Mado, she got through the darkness. She knowed love has to work itself all the way through the dark feelings; you can't go 'round them; they has to be gone through, all the way through.[4]

Name as many examples of suffering as you can. "They has to be gone through, all the way through," until we come out into the glowing light of glory. This is true whether we are naming specific forms that suffering takes, or the more general description given to us in Romans 5 and 8. We go all the way accompanied by Jesus Christ, the wounded Healer. And we are even now being transformed from one degree of glory to another, though we don't notice. We don't know the half of what that glory will finally be (2 Cor. 3:18; 4:6–18;

1 Cor. 2:8–10). We know the merest bit and only a fraction of that!

Perhaps we would know more if we lived intimately with nature and observed winter as David and Virginia Owens did. She writes of how we

> exempt ourselves from the season of death that envelops the world outside our artificial environment. . . . Maybe, watching the world die, I could learn to enter into that absolute still center at the heart of the universe, the death of Christ, where I could leave everything behind.[5]

We don't want to touch the actuality of Jesus' death any more than I wanted to touch my father as he lay in the casket. But an "absolute still center" stands at the heart of the universe, at the center of Scripture, at the core of Romans, and at the root of Romans 5:1–11. We must handle this truth: The Lord Christ died.

When we were still powerless, Christ died for the ungodly—us. Accused, mocked, flogged, and bruised, he was also slapped and stripped. He endured sarcasm, insult, thorns, and thirst. The saliva of others was on his face. Finally, he endured crucifixion.

God demonstrated his own love for us in this: While we were still sinners, Christ went through rejection, betrayal, loneliness, anguish, mental suffering, emotional torture, and physical agony—"a killing sense of human malice and callousness, and a horror of great spiritual darkness."[6] Finally, death, that ultimate, final extreme of all pain.

> He deliberately drained dry the vinegar of suffering. . . .
> Caught by the nails . . . Jesus moved steadfastly through his Calvary to the thoroughgoing acceptance of it all, the deadly accurate hammer strokes of sin embraced not deflected. . . .

The nails in his hands burned like pieces of molten silver, pure pain. That was the cost. Purchasing forgiveness has its own unalloyed price.[7]

There is utter silence now; there is no music here. Wordlessly I enter that absolute still center at the heart of the universe, recognizing the reality of Christ's death, his death for me. He was delivered over to death for my sins and raised to life for my justification.

Therefore . . . peace. In him there is peace. In him there is hope. Reconciled through his death, I am saved through his life.[8]

Grasping something of the necessity of his suffering and death, I can no longer seek an artificial environment to exempt myself from pain. Refusing to hibernate in a warm, protected den throughout wintry blasts doesn't mean that I go out to seek pain, but that when suffering comes, I learn to accept its necessity.

And by a miracle of grace, in the presence of the slain Lamb—the stricken Shepherd, the wounded Healer—in the presence of the risen Christ, I come out on the other side.[9] I am accompanied all the way by a Companion who was abandoned, so that I would never know that abandonment. I am accompanied by an experienced Guide who knows the way. I lean on Christ whose resurrection canceled the dead of winter. I come out into the warmth of the hope of glory.

Rhythms
of Expectancy

The sons of God will stand forth revealed in the glories of their bright inheritance. And for that consummation . . . creation, both animate and inanimate, waits with eager longing; like spectators straining forward over the ropes to catch the first glimpse of some triumphal pageant.

William Sanday and Arthur Headlam

This conjunction of death and life, of suffering and resurrection, is not . . . a program that one could automatically follow; it is, with all the knowledge of Christ, a wrestling, a stretching out with every effort of the soul toward that which has not yet been attained.

Herman Ridderbos

Faith for Paul . . . is not only trust . . . but the ability to sustain the contradiction between present reality and future hope, and to live out of that tension.

J. Christiaan Beker

9

Suffering, a Sacred Situation

"God, I understand that Christ suffered, and so must I. But isn't there some other way, some easier way for those whom I love? Couldn't you keep their security intact, perhaps with a specially built dome, the controlled environment of a perpetual springtime?" Arctic winters are not kind, and I find it extremely difficult to allow God the freedom to dictate weather forecasts in the lives of those who have my affection. What would *seem at first* to be injurious I find almost impossible to allow.

I have seen these so-called blizzards in the lives of those whom I would pamper. At Christmas 1986 I sat with Jim and Rebecca at a concert, nearly two years after they had lost Carol. She had gone abruptly with a coronary attack. They had experienced sudden sorrow, a massive loss, yet they had faced their grief head-on. When I came on the scene later, I began to feel their loss, too.

As we sat listening to a superb performance of Handel's *Messiah*, I had already shared enough of their grief to respond with deep feeling when the soloist sang, "He was a man of sorrows and acquainted with grief." Christ was familiar with grief; he was well schooled by grief, and he carried our sorrows. My having shared Jim and Rebecca's sorrows had given me the flavor, a taste of what Scripture means when it says that Jesus Christ bore our griefs and carried our sorrows (Isa. 53). He not only carries our sorrows, he carries us, as a shepherd carries his sheep (Isa. 53:3–4; 40:11) and he transforms suffering.

With Jim and Rebecca in mind, I listened to the music as truth poured out before us. This truth ranged from our sinfulness to our forgiveness; from the tender "comfort ye" to the excruciating "he was despised"; from sorrow to "hallelujah"; from the silence of death to the sounding of the resurrection. The music expressed a taste of pain and foretastes of glory. But Jim and Rebecca knew more than the taste of sorrow, and I could not minimize the choking swallow, the bitterness of the taste, nor the stale aftereffects.

It helped me immensely, as I felt their sorrow, to know that they knew God, and that they were getting to know him more fully through their pain. Could I apply Paul's words in Romans 5 to accompany them through the grief that remained? Yes. Why? Because Paul's term for suffering (*thlipsis*) is meant to be applied in a broad sense—not just for the first century, not just for Christian martyrs, not just for the church staff here, not just for missionaries in distant cultures.

The specific Greek term, *thlipsis*, covers the whole catalog of human distress, and is used often with synonyms for inward pain. In the New Testament, *thlipsis* is affliction related to external pressures, and could also be used of the crush of a thronging crowd (Mark 3:9). Even the sound of *thlipsis* reminds me that it originally referred to squeezing a grape.

We are all reluctant to be pressed out into fine wine. When we begin to feel the pressure of pain, whether it comes from external situations or turmoil that we create within ourselves, we say, "I don't need this." If possible, we dodge around, jump over, or tunnel under the difficulty. We shrink from being squeezed. We do anything to prevent ourselves from being trodden on, pressed, and poured out as wine. From whom can we learn to approach the unavoidable winepresses we face? We learn from the only one whose suffering surpasses all other.

Our Lord was stomped on, pressed, and poured out as wine for us. Isaiah predicted that he would be crushed for our iniquities, and even that it was God's will that he be crushed and that he suffer. But Isaiah also said, "After the suffering of his soul, he will see the light of life and be satisfied . . ." (Isa. 53:5, 10, 11). The pattern of light after darkness, and life after death, holds for us as it did for Christ. Both the Old and the New Testaments assure and reassure us of this truth.

When the Old Testament was translated from Hebrew into Greek, *thlipsis* was the word chosen for passages telling of dangerous risks, hostility, homesickness, abandonment, oppression, mockery by enemies, and physical injuries and illnesses. The word is used of Jacob's distress in fleeing Esau, of Joseph's turmoil when he pleaded with his brothers against their selling him to foreigners, and of Hannah in her childlessness.

In reading about Hannah, perhaps you have been angry with her rival, Peninnah, as I have been (1 Sam. 1). Peninnah was an award-winning instigator of *thlipsis* if ever there was one. There she was with all her sons and daughters, and Hannah with none. Fertile in her mind as well as her body, Peninnah decided to inflict a deep thorn of *thlipsis*, driving it home that *she* had given Elkanah children, while Hannah, who wanted children so badly, had not. Insensitive, aggravating Peninnah! Not only did she pull this again and again, year after year, but she kept it up until Hannah was in such distress that she couldn't eat. And Peninnah did this at the house of the Lord during sacrifice time. She embarrassed herself through all of history by hurting Hannah and by taking the credit for God's having opened her womb.

Wouldn't you have liked to have seen Peninnah's face when the news spread that Hannah was pregnant? So much for her *thlipsis* campaign! I wonder what her attitude was when Samuel was born? What did she think when Hannah gave Samuel to God? What did she think when Samuel became a statesman, bringing God's word to all Israel? What did she think when Samuel became known and respected everywhere?

I can identify with Hannah. I too, have wept much and prayed as she did in 1 Samuel 1:11. "Lord Almighty, look upon your servant's misery and remember me. Give me children, and I'll give them back to you." God gave Hannah a son, Samuel, whom she dedicated to him, along with three more sons and two daughters.

Of course, there are many differences between Hannah and me. Samuel was to have a particular place in Israel's history, in redemptive history. But the fact remains: Hannah prayed and then had sons and daughters. I prayed and did not.

This was my private agenda for studying the relationship of suffering and hope in Romans. Could I use *thlipsis* broadly to include any kind of pain, even emotional pain? Could I apply it to twentieth-century childlessness? Could I anticipate that this particular sort of suffering might give birth to hope? Could I hope that, if not free from the desire for children, I might be free from the *tyranny* of the desire, free from the anguish of menopausal finality? Yes—praise and thank God, a fourfold yes.

Over the four summers of my academic study of Romans, the truth took up more and more space in my intellect. That was a strong start. In the years since completing the thesis, I've invited the truth to connect with my will, and at last, have allowed it to move in on my emotions. I have come to trust God's sovereign control on both sides of the story, Hannah's and mine; those with children and those without.

You are perhaps wondering what role my stepdaughter, Rebecca, has played. At the beginning of my engagement to Jim, I decided not to anticipate her filling a daughter's role for me. Rebecca was eighteen at that time, and only a few months removed from her mother's funeral—not good timing for my presenting myself as the answer to a step-daughter's dream. I wrote from Canada, telling her that I hoped to be her friend but that the relational moves would have to originate with her, and proceed at her pace. I sup-pose I was being self-protective. After all, why go out look-ing for hurt, trying to find brick walls to bang my head against? In those early days (quite early for a grieving daughter), Rebecca was understandably reluctant. She was caught between loyalty to her absent mother and a desire for her dad's happiness. She chose to live for the living.

Her brick walls proved to be as substantial as the sand-castle walls she had built on the beach as a child. I did not come in like an ocean at full tide to dissolve them. But as a gentle mist over time . . . a slow melt of soft barriers. . . . Carol had unknowingly done me a favor in helping Jim pro-duce an emotionally healthy young woman who was courte-ous to me even before I earned her trust. I owe Carol a great deal, and am thankful to her.

A year and a half after Carol's death, Jim and I married, and I had to pin my arms at my sides in order not to hug Rebecca before she was ready. I am naturally more like an ocean with barely perceptible low tides, and for me the gen-tle-mist approach required God's Spirit for my self-control. By the end of a year, Rebecca and I were way ahead of my hoped-for schedule, and by the time of her own marriage just after our third anniversary, she did everything in her power to make me feel like a card-carrying mother of the bride.

She and I say to one another that God has allowed us reciprocal healing. Rebecca lost her mother, but was given me. I had been expecting a child since my girlhood, and was given Rebecca. But we both know that I will never be her mother, and she is not my child. We are friends.

I must say here of Rebecca something I said earlier of Jim. I cannot hang on her the heavy task of meeting needs that only God can handle. Yes, she is a joy to my heart, and I am about as proud of her as a mother might be. But I know that God is everything. I realize that no relationship other than a Godward one can claim to fully meet a canyon-deep need.

Learning to trust him for contentment meant freedom from envy, my envy of modern-day Hannahs. I looked to God for help in identifying and handling pure pain, as opposed to pain plus self-pity, pain plus envy, or pain plus anger. Then I looked to God for help with self-pity, envy, and anger, as separate problems. I asked God for rest and for peace as *he* would define rest and peace for the childless, and requested his application of resurrection power to an intimate, personal ache. God and I made a contract that every time I saw an obviously pregnant woman, I would glance inwardly to him and say, "My body is yours. Yes, God, my body is yours to do with as you will."

Does God's application of resurrection power mean that all the barrenness is behind me? No, but the tyranny of its emptiness is past; the engulfing sadness is gone. God is a God of fullness, a God of life. And I am enabled sometimes by him to take joy in the thriving of new life. If not joy, then love, as I borrow his love to replace envy and give me pleasure in their happiness. If not emotions of joy and love, then a chosen mental love, and thankfulness for God's perfect oversight and direction in my life. I am grateful for all the ministry opportunities I've had that my having children would have prevented. My thoughts go to God who spells contentment for me in dozens of ways. Now I know the paths through this wilderness, and can make mental tracks more quickly into peace. He satisfies my desires with good things (Ps. 103:5).

For contemporary *thlipsis* and up-to-date hope, you have my very personal word that Romans 5 applies. *Thlipsis* pain can become a sacred situation, and suffering is first manageable and then often curable. The cure is not always immediate.

David used the word *thlipsis* in passages about needing deliverance when facing his enemies. Oppression and suffering are often linked with deliverance in the Old Testament, *with the suffering considered as meaningful as the deliverance itself.*[1]

David spoke of "a spacious place," when describing the welcomed deliverance from the pressured circumstances of *thlipsis*. Kathryn Koob, a Christian American hostage freed by Iran in 1981, followed the psalmists' model, focusing on God and looking to him during the ordeal for daily help, for relief, and for long-range outcomes. Miss Koob was in complete isolation for 120 days of the 444 days that she was held hostage. Setting a schedule of prayer and meditation, she made no bargains with God, but thanked him for each new day. Literally pressed by outside circumstances and tangible walls, she experienced *thlipsis*; one can imagine the significance of her reading Psalms that centered on God, and her praising when she regained a physically spacious "cell."[2]

> He rescued me from my powerful enemy. . . .
> He brought me out into a spacious place;
>   he rescued me because he delighted in me.
>   Psalm 18:17, 19

> Though you have made me see troubles, many and bitter,
>   you will restore my life again;
> from the depths of the earth
>   you will again bring me up.
> You will increase my honor
>   and comfort me once again.
>   Psalm 71:20–21

Before I was afflicted I went astray,
    but now I obey your word. . . .
in faithfulness you have afflicted me.

                                        Psalm 119:67, 75

In my anguish I cried to the LORD,
    and he answered by setting me free [i.e., bringing me into
    a wide place].

                                            Psalm 118:5

Praise our God . . .
he has preserved our lives . . .
For you, O God, tested us;
    you refined us like silver.
You brought us into prison
    and laid burdens on our backs.
You let men ride over our heads;
    we went through fire and water,
    but you brought us to a place of abundance.

                                         Psalm 66:8–12

In speaking of testing and of burdens, Psalm 66 anticipates
the vocabulary chosen later by Paul, and we find the New
Testament applying the same diversity to the term *thlipsis*:
the word Paul chose in writing about the God of all comfort
who comforts us in all our *troubles*. He also uses it in describing the *hardships* of great pressure in Asia that caused
him to despair of life. He wrote Second Corinthians out of
great *distress* and anguish of heart and refers to a *harassing*
time in Macedonia with conflicts outside and fears within
(2 Cor. 1:4, 8; 2:4; 7:5). Each time, his word of choice is
thlipsis.

Persecution, imprisonment, extreme poverty, the distress
of widows and orphans, fear, the pain of childbirth, famine,
sorrow, anguish—all relate to the word *thlipsis* in the New
Testament.[3] Of course, there are other words used as synonyms, and other words Paul could have chosen, but what
we have seen here is sufficient to show us that the "*thlipsis*
suffering" in Romans 5, this pain that causes hope to grow,

includes the wide range of human distress.[4] I say that *not* just because of the word's general meaning but also because Paul does not limit the word in the Romans passage that we are reading.

You and I may pray for *thlipsis*-producing hope as we think of our fellow Christians: a widow crowded by the hard reality of her husband's suicide; an executive whose business folds, caught in a collision of her own expectations and those of the board of directors; survivors of divorce, bombarded by unwelcome memories; a man after surgery, facing the necessity and side-effects of chemotherapy; as well as unemployment, dysfunctional families, and urban riots. Such concerns and threats send us to Psalm 94: "When anxiety was great within me, your consolation brought joy to my soul" (v. 19).

Suffering is a sacred situation, a set-apart time for searching out God's love.[5] Suffering of every kind can serve as the sacred event that stimulates conversation with God. I look back on my own pain as occasions for bowing inwardly, awaiting God's tender touch. He comes. I am changed.

What or who can separate us from the love of Christ? Small *thlipsis* or hardship or persecution or famine or nakedness or danger or sword? No, in all these things we may be more than conquerors through him who loves us . . . Neither death nor life, neither angels nor demons, neither the present nor the future, nor any powers, neither height nor depth, nor *anything else* in all creation will be able to separate us from the love of God that is in Christ Jesus our Lord (adapted from Rom. 8:35–39).

10

Frustration's Goal: Freedom at Last

"Ahhh'g'rl. Amen." Once when I had a cold and a cough, Ric and I talked by phone, but I could not catch the sound, "Ahhh'g'rl." His mother translated for me. He had turned to God, saying only his nickname for me, and his version of "amen," a prayer for my health.

"Nothing can separate us from the love of Christ." Truth for a conqueror named Ric who walks in the love of God but cannot tell you about it—at least, not verbally. In his thirties, Ric uses a few words like "bye-bye," "man," "foo'ball," and "car." But most vocabulary was lost in his early development, and Ric depends on nonverbal skills in order to communicate. Someone has said that he is a bit like a snowflake because there is not another like him. With a memory better than most adults, affection and sensitivity beyond that of some executives I know, barely harnessed energy that I envy, and a laugh that happily infects others, Ric is my good friend.

Years ago Ric's pastor lost his daughter due to a brain tumor. On the Sunday after the funeral, most adults were at a loss when they shook the minister's hand at the church door. Ric's response, however, was the most appropriate of all. He traced lines down his face where tears would roll and then patted his own shoulder, indicating, "You can cry right here, Pastor. I want to comfort you."

Ric and his family bring a breadth of theology to apply to their frustration every day. Their faith is lived out. His parents have written that they've experienced a miracle greater than healing, a miracle called coping.[1] It is not easy. To me, Ric's life represents the ultimate in frustration; his having so much to offer, but lacking the major channel for letting us know what it is!

Ric has a special role: A believer living an entire lifetime in perpetual, unchanging frustration, he is a unique messenger of hope. Ric's life is a metaphor for existence. None of us are able to fulfill the goals of glorifying God as was originally intended at creation. Although not as obvious to the human eye as is Ric's situation, the whole of creation is subjected to frustration in a way that is parallel to Ric's: We are frustrated in an almost infinite catalog of experiences, which makes us long intensely for the redemption of our bodies.

Frustration, suffering, hope, glory; Paul hasn't dropped a stitch in his close-knit lesson. And borrowing his words, we may respond, "If God is for us, who can be against us? He who did not spare his own Son, but gave him up for us all— how will he not also, along with him, graciously give us all things?" (Rom. 8:31–32).

God is for us. Romans 5:1–11 is only one of a pair of sturdy, nonsliding bookends, the matching piece being found in Romans 8:17–30. When I was in Africa, I had the fun of purchasing some beautiful wooden bookends for friends in Michigan, and Romans 5 and 8 remind me of those bookends. They were full of character, worth studying, with notches and markings in the reddish brown wood that was polished on the outer surfaces but unpolished on the inner surfaces. They were substantial, and wouldn't allow books to slide no matter how determined or slippery the books seemed.

Paul's brief statement in Romans 5 on the certainty of salvation, including the solid hope of glory produced by suffering, is expanded in the eighth chapter. In Romans 8, Paul creates a tremendous sense of anticipation and excited expectancy as the believer and creation await the glory that will finally be revealed (Rom. 8:20). Remember that creation is waiting, at this very moment subjected to frustration in hope. I think you will agree that frustration is a form of suffering. Although people, in this passage, are set apart from "creation," it is true that both nonhuman and human creation are frustrated in their attempts to display God's glory as first intended. One difference is that the nonhuman element, the universe, waits unconsciously to glorify him fully, while humans may progress by intelligent choice to glorify him.

The term *frustration*, along with its close relatives, appears eleven times in the New Testament, with slightly different shades of meaning, applicable to that which is futile, empty, or vain. People apart from God became futile in their thinking (Rom. 1:21; Eph. 4:17). In Romans 8, we read that believers and creation will finally and fully participate in God's glory, though to do so now seems impossible. In this context the best meaning for *frustration* is "that which does not reach its goal."

Within this word *frustration* is the idea of looking for something that one is unable to find. Remember the last time you lost your keys, and hunted everywhere—and you were already late? This is but a minor, yet annoying, frantic frustration! You may name other frustrations of far greater magnitude. I, of course, think of the frustration of being programmed convincingly with the goals of marriage and motherhood, preferably achieved by age twenty-five. Nothing had ever been offered me as a valuable alternative. Not even my consistent successes in adulthood could cancel my feeling of failure in these areas. I am still sensitive on the behalf of women who are being pushed toward marriage only.

For me, singleness extended for an extra twenty-two years beyond college. By then menopause had turned childbearing into a megagoal that I could not reach. A large measure of freedom finally came when I was at long last able to sincerely say to God, "My body is yours." Like me, like Ric, and like others around us, creation is caught in frustration, but Romans 8:20 tells us that frustration is *in hope until* there is liberation into *glorious freedom*.

On a universal, grand scale, creation waits to glorify God totally. It waits as if on tiptoe with neck outstretched scanning the horizon, looking for fulfillment, waiting for the immeasurable glorious freedom that will one day come.

Frustration is a temporary affliction for the children of God, whether it is the frustration of our wanting to bring him more glory now but realizing our inability, or the more concrete, down-to-earth frustrations of loss or of physical inadequacy and limitations. The frustration and grief of a widow's finding she has set two places at the table, and then remembering only one is needed; the frustration of a disabled adult like Ric, who sees others drive to work while he waits every day for a bus to the sheltered workshop; the heavy frustration of a rape victim, who is unable to communicate with the policeman on duty. These are horrid, real, and concrete frustrations, sometimes past describing.

"God is frustrating." Yesterday I sat with a group of twenty college students as we took turns affirming each other and God. Each person gave a word describing the people on his or her left and right in a way that would encourage the others. After that, each one affirmed God. Many said that God is their comfort, their support, their strength. One person said, "God is always there and nudging me"; another, "I am glad that God isn't angry." Then we came to Barry, who said, "God is frustrating."

Vulnerably and honestly, Barry told us how frustrating he finds God to be right now because of what is happening to his friend, Don. After major back surgery following several years of pain, and now just a few weeks before his wedding, Don has a slipped disc. Understandably, to Barry and others in relationship with Don, God appears to be a fickle frustrator. But he only appears that way, and only for now.

Without minimizing the pain, Paul reminds us in Romans that Christians are not stuck forever under frustration. There are answers, and there is relief, as Scripture is applied over the long haul. Romans 8 tells us that creation is not fenced in or enslaved to frustration forever. The hope of release is a well-founded waiting for full relief. Frustration has a beginning and an end; "before its beginning and beyond its end is God."[2]

Throughout this passage Paul works quite hard to build contrasts: Frustration and "bondage to decay" are extended preambles to hope and freedom; present suffering is an overture to future glory; active waiting parallels patience in faithful waiting; "groans" are actually positive longings expressed as anticipatory sighs.

Both the groaning as in the pains of childbirth and the groaning as we wait eagerly (Rom. 8:22–23), are positive sounds that emerge from an eager heart, from the heart of someone focused on a longed-for joy. These are the sorts of happy emissions we hear from children just before a holiday, or from a child-at-heart en route to greet a friend, or from a groom when he finally has his bride at his side. Paul gives us an intertwined mixture of eager anticipation and patient waiting, of momentary suffering and an eternal weight of future glory; and he maintains this creative tension throughout the passage.

Paul is a master at building spiritual tension in words, at creating suspense on the page. And at the end of verse twenty-three, we find that Paul hasn't finished with us yet. He mentions yet another variety of pain in verse twenty-six, when he brings in our "weakness." The groans and sighs of the creation and of the believer are future oriented, but those of the Spirit occur now as he comes to our aid because we are weak. The family of terms related to *weakness* covers "the full range of physical, emotional, social, economic, and even spiritual incapacity."[3] Covering just about everything, it includes Karen's physical weaknesses, Rev. Mac's fatal weakness, Ric's developmental weakness, all of your weaknesses and all of mine. This particular word for weakness occurs in the Gospels to describe physical problems, but is used often by Paul, more widely. While comprehensiveness of the word could embrace all the weaknesses of our lives, in Romans 8:26 it is limited to our weakness in prayer. Although our prayers may seem to line up with God's wisdom, love, and grace, in actuality they may not; you and I need the Spirit's help to turn prayer weakness into strength and to ask for that which is "good" from God's perspective.

"All things" do not simply mix together "for good," without God's chemistry (Rom. 8:28). The phrase, *all things*, includes the "present sufferings" of Romans 8:18 and the concrete ones mentioned in verses thirty-five through thirty-nine. All things, even those that seem adverse or hurtful—persecution, death, famine—all things work *together* for good. God causes Ric, with all his limitations and with little vocabulary, to bring him glory. Do we accept that our God is that phenomenal a chemist?

How do you use the word *good*? It would be *good* if the daffodil bulbs get enough rain. This chocolate candy is very *good*. I'll feel *good* when I get a break from work. Romans 8 has its own definition. Verse twenty-nine is linked closely to the previous verse by the little word *for*. We must read on to discover that conformity to the likeness of Christ is a part of "the good." That which is good does not stem from a vague notion that "God's in his heaven, and all's right with the world," or a fond wish that "things will turn out all right," or a casual "somebody up there loves you." The good is not the same as comfort, consumerism, and convenience—the ease we choose when we prefer quick, early gratification. *Good* includes all things that assist our salvation. It includes the entire section of Romans 8 with its strong theme of glory, and its concepts of adoption, conformity to Christ's image, redemption, and the totality of God's purposes—an overload of "goods" that would blow our so-called spiritual fuses if we understood them all.

And finally, we will be "glorified."

For those of us who believe, including Ric, there will, at last, be participation in the freedom of glory. Articulately and beautifully, Ric will sing in heaven. Those whom Christ justified, he will also glorify, throughout suffering and after suffering. There will be a marvelous "after," when he will wipe every tear from our eyes. "There will be no more death or mourning or crying or pain, for the old order of things" will have passed away (Rev. 21:4).

Graciously God gives us all things (Rom. 8:32), including frustration, which will spill out into freedom from such suffering. Too good to be true, this is nonetheless factual.

11

The Pause That Progresses

"Was God gracious? Oh, yes, throughout all of our grieving. But it was after someone said that I wouldn't make progress until I stopped asking, 'Why?' that he freed me from the densest grief, the most acute pain." Hildy's sixteen-year-old daughter, Carrie, had died when the car in which she was a passenger collided with a truck on an icy road. She had run back inside their home at the last minute that day to get her coat, saying she might need it. The coat was used to cover her body at the roadside.

Four months earlier, on New Year's Eve, Carrie had stood during a service at church to read to the congregation, "I eagerly expect and hope that . . . Christ will be exalted in my body whether by life or by death. For to me, to live is Christ, and to die is gain" (Phil. 1:20–21). A sword had pierced Hildy's heart when she heard Carrie read with such convic-

tion, and she inwardly realized the importance of relinquishing such a daughter to God for his good purposes. She
began to value more than anything the perfect choices of God
in her own life, as well as in her family's. She had been prepared gently by God in daily prayer times for the news, "There
has been an accident. Your daughter is dead."

The valley of the shadow of death, the wilderness, the
desert, the fog—all images of the bleakness we feel at death,
and particularly at the death of a young person. Peter and
Hildy are parents who, because of their daughter's death,
began a pilgrimage, and fourteen years later, Christ is exalted in many lives because of it. The young people who were
close to Carrie at the time of her death are now all committed to Christian vocations. Carrie's parents know that to be
with Christ in person has been gain for Carrie. As Hildy told
me the story, I could see that her early trust had moved and
had developed into peace.

A pilgrimage means movement. In the dry, cracked desert,
when our canteens are dusty even on the inside, we will try
desperately to find water by searching out water-storing
plants; by looking for hidden sources, springs or an unlikely
trickling stream; or by praying for dew or rain. In Psalm 84,
the Valley of Baca means either a "thirsty valley" where trees
and shrubs grow in arid, parched conditions, or a "Valley of
Weeping," so-called because of certain trees that "weep" or
exude moisture. People like Hildy and Peter, who have set
their hearts on a pilgrimage, make either kind of valley a place
of springs. In pilgrimage we move even when it seems we are
standing still.

Modern-day pilgrims, as we saw in the last chapter, choose
to set their hearts on what's ahead, and they themselves decide to look actively for springs; God's part is to point out
hidden water or provide obvious rain. Such pilgrims go on
from strength to even more strength "till each appears before God." This Old Testament picture links with the New
Testament where we read that believers move from glory to

even more glory, until they see Christ as he is and become like him, transformed into his image.[1]

In pain, we feel like trudging and slogging along. We may feel like giving up and stopping. The people who are *passing through* the Valley of Baca do *not* trudge grudgingly along the dunes planning to build homes in the "thirsty valley." There is movement *through* the wilderness and movement *out* of it; it is unusual for the Christian to stay there interminably. Pilgrims have a Guide.

The desert or wilderness is meant to be a temporary location. But *temporary* is a relative term, and can actually cover a long period of time. Time becomes a blur. It seems that if the "clock" on our emotions is ever going to stop, it will be in the middle of affliction. This imaginary clock always reads a quarter past the hour of hurt. Movement through time is imperceptible. Oh, God of vast deserts and wildernesses, of seemingly stopped watches, God of our dreary Bacavilles, give us patience!

He replies, "I will."

Suffering produces patience.

Patience in the Old Testament relates directly to waiting, especially to Israel's waiting on God in all the ups and downs of her covenant relationship with him. What do we twentieth-century pilgrims know about waiting? Or about patience?

One of my elementary-school teachers told us that when we wait, it means we have found someone more important than ourselves. As a child I found no one more important than myself, and I puzzled over her comment for a long time. I know now what she meant. When I am waiting for someone who is significant to me, someone who has become more important than self, I am quite willing to wait; to freely give such a person my minutes, hours, or days tied up with a ribbon. I may become restless at times, yes, but don't dare try to move me when I have decided this person is worth the wait!

The anticipation of their coming makes it almost impossible to sit still. Every muffled sound must be the car door and I am pulled to the window to check again. You know, don't you, that energetic excitement growing from the happy certainty that a friend is about to arrive? When we were engaged, that energetic excitement took Jim to the airport hours before my plane was due, and moved me up four rows to be just that much closer to the exit, much to the flight attendant's surprise. In anticipation my feelings had arrived at the airport well ahead of my body, so I had to endure the indulgent smiles of people around me.

What do any of us know about anticipating or waiting *on* and *for* God? Waiting spiritually means I have found Someone more important than myself, and I must maintain an attitude of readiness for contact with him just as determinedly as I maintained my riveted position when I was waiting to get off the airplane. I must hold spiritual ground just as steadily as I hold my place near our front door when the mailman is coming with a special letter. All day, every day, I must wait on God for resources, even when the circumstances are not happy; especially when the circumstances are not happy.

But there is a difference between the expectancy of active *patience* and the striving of active *impatience*. In my spiritual life, active patience or perseverance focuses on God, awaiting his provision of grace, calmness, strength, quietness, and relief at last. It is a preoccupation with God.

Active impatience whimpers, writhes, and struggles, focusing on the problem and the pain. A preoccupation with God prevents total occupation with the difficulty, a tiring absorption in the negative aspects of the scene. Itchy impatience is the natural, not the supernatural, result of tribulation. Healthy, active patience is supernatural; it will not thrive in the unbeliever, nor will it grow well in the believer whose focus is earthbound.[2]

Biblical patience or perseverance is energetic fortitude, the opposite of passive quietness and withdrawal. It is resistance to pressure, bearing up without abjectly giving in with sagging posture and a dull, limp spirit. An exercised, cooperative, communicative spirit reaches out toward God.

Perseverance may include waiting (and waiting and waiting) with an acquired and growing calm, but it also reaches eagerly forward to God and to what he offers in the situation. This is waiting not only for relief, but also *for God*, whose person and ways are more important than my own schemes and methods. There is progress in the pause. *Waiting on God can become as significant as the desired relief.*

Why is the wait so significant? Why does God insist on the delay? The pause, the enforced waiting, is absolutely essential so that our *values* have time to undergo a crucial change. Our values quite easily attach to people, relationships, goals, jobs, possessions, comfort, security, and happy circumstances like a cup of coffee by the fire with a friend on a rainy day, a challenging task in a profitable job, or staying healthy until retirement in wealth. I turn elements like these into gods. "A god is a center of value by which other values are judged."[3] I elevate limited values to "ultimate givers of meaning," and it happens again and again, even when I think the lesson has been learned. Virginia Stem Owens tantalizes me as she writes of this lesson. She reflected through a long Wyoming winter:

> Maybe . . . mute lessons would seep slowly into the landscape of my mind, so that I could learn to bear the abandonment of my own life. Maybe, watching the world die, I could learn to enter into that absolute still center at the heart of the universe, the death of Christ, where I could leave everything behind.[4]

To leave our "gods" behind is our goal as maturing Christians. When Hildy heard Carrie read those verses on New Year's Eve, she shivered with the knowledge that God might ask her to put his choice above her own preferences. She

feared that God might present her with a painful privilege—
the fellowship of his sufferings. In the four months between
Carrie's testimony on New Year's Eve and the accident in
April, God helped Hildy begin to release Carrie to himself.

There seems to be no inborn immunity from our habit of
turning people or "things" into gods. We are all susceptible,
and we need waiting periods, pauses, times for reevaluating
our sources of meaning. I find myself trying for example, to
make my husband an ultimate giver of meaning—a heavy
role to force on any human being. The result is guilt, and
whether recognized as such or not, whether labeled as "suffering" or not, guilt is a form of human pain. Guilt is the result of my placing anything or anyone into first place, the
place reserved by God for himself. God alone can fill that
prime position, and not wanting us burdened with such guilt,
he will go to unmeasured lengths to relieve us of it. God gives
us pauses for "proportional valuing" because he wants us to
be guilt free.[5] Freedom from guilt only comes when we are
as God-centered as we know how to be.

Fear and its accompanying anxiety are also a type of suffering. The things we value, that give meaning to our lives,
can also be what bring us fear. I work at gaining and maintaining freedom from the fear of losing Jim to a white, gelati-
nous rope in his arteries called cholesterol. At the grocery
store, I probably look like an intelligent consumer, a good
homemaker, a gourmet cook, or a ridiculously avid reader.
I am actually shopping under the influence of fear. Beneath
the exterior of an adult in control, I can be a scared little girl.
Palm oil, eggs, butter, red meat: poisons with the invisible
stamp of a skull and crossbones. I will do everything this side
of usurping God's sovereignty to keep Jim on earth with me.
"God, do you ever loan sovereignty, and if so, how do you
measure it out? May I borrow a sufficient amount of fat-free
sovereignty, please, to apply to Jim's body? Just a little, or is
it many miles worth of your power that I need to sweep clean
the curbs of his arteries? Is the control I want measured in

years? Forty more years' worth, okay, God? Oh. You say power and control are yours? What? Am I trying to be God again?"

Every now and then, we have it out, God and I. And I end up waiting before God; waiting on God. "Yes, Jim *is* yours. No, keeping him here beyond his due date isn't my job. Yes, bringing home the right food is. I want him only as long as you say. Yes, I know you will be here whether or not he is." And after a while, maybe a long while . . . "Yes, my Lord and my God, yes . . . you are first." Spiritual chemotherapy has shrunk my fear, halting the consuming growth that eats at my health.

I am like our collie-shepherd in two respects. Tula knows devotion to me, and he also knows fear. I know devotion to God, and I know fear, too. When I take Tula for walks and we come to the footbridge for crossing Deerfield Road, traffic moves steadily below. We see and hear it. On the right of the footbridge is a barrier to protect us from stumbling onto train tracks or into a moving train, and on our left is a fence to prevent our falling onto the cars below. Tula, who until now has been moving along at an exuberant frisky pace, suddenly becomes timid. Devoted to me, ready to do my will, but afraid. He hunkers down, reducing his height by a good six inches. He hugs the bridge, his massive white paws splayed out to their fullest for maximum balance. He whispers a whimper. His eyes glance quickly from side to side, and he moves as close to me as he can, barely allowing us to move. Once we have crossed the bridge and the ordeal is over, he gains majestic height quite quickly, happiness and dignity in canine motion. "Me? Afraid? I'm a *big* dog."

And so, if I come to a footbridge with God, someday without Jim . . . I know I will need to work hard at keeping my balance. I may even lose my balance, falling on him. I will cry. I will be afraid. But I know God. My devotion and trust are well placed. I have known aloneness with him, and when I think it through, I know from the past that his bridges make sense. Fear of the bridge is worse than the bridge itself, because fear robs me of time and energy in the "now." My fear is more subtle than my grief but has the potential to be equally paralyzing. I have a choice, and I will not allow fear's hostile takeover. God can reason with me and grant me freedom. I am not a dog.

Freedom from guilt, freedom from fear, and freedom from their binding tyranny enables me to enjoy life in the present. I am not depleted of energy. Important spiritual work is accomplished as I wait on God in times of thoughtful reflection, regardless of the kind of pain and regardless of whether others would agree to name it suffering. This spiritual work is "progress" during the pause. Although we have no gauge or gadget for measuring our advance, it is nonetheless real.

As I lean on God, I receive a lesson in proportional valuing. During the four months between Carrie's testimony and her death, Hildy began to learn a right sort of cherishing that did not make the loss any easier, only more endurable. This was a process, which required time. God will always bring me to admit the limitations of my "gods," legitimate and good only when assessed correctly as limited values. While they are immensely valuable, and I treasure and cherish them, proportional valuing means that God is the ultimate giver of meaning. Hildy knew that with deep knowing.

Being deprived of temporal supports that have given earthly happiness enables us to understand God's place and enjoy sweetness when he fills it. This does not mean that spouses, children, friends, goals, and such, have no place; it means that they are thoroughly enjoyed, even treasured, only in the right place. These are some of the truths we learn at deeper levels while we wait, if indeed we wait *on God*. Waiting on God truly does become as significant as the desired relief.

I found that hard to say a few months ago, because I had just heard from Karen, who in addition to her multiple sclerosis, partial sight, recent meningitis, miscarriage, and

rheumatoid arthritis, had been abandoned by her husband
for an extended time, left with three children and little money.
She writes, "I would gladly trade in some future glory for
some present peace." Who among us has not felt that desire,
and if we could put it as clearly, would not have said the
same? Please God, one tiny wrinkle in eternity for a moment
of smoothness now, or please, a magic wand to boost us over
the bad patch.

> Magic wands to get us over the hard parts are not the same
> as death and resurrection. If I want the self-I-am brought to
> fruition, it must be squeezed and scraped through the nar-
> row birth-gate of our obedience that includes dying . . . I
> would prefer . . . obliteration—to the hard dying I am called
> to. I am a coward.[6]

We are given no magic wand. We are expected to be obedient, perhaps with abrasions, but still obedient, and that requires waiting on God, lest we give in to our cowardice.

I must wait on God with Karen. I must wait on God *for*
her, and it may be hard work, like removing pieces of roof
so that a sick person can be lowered to the feet of Christ.
Waiting on God with and for Karen, "placing her at the feet
of Christ," are ways of saying that I must pray, that something deep in my soul cries out to him when I think of her.

I would like to pray for the easy thing: relief. And I do. I
ask for healing, for reconciliation in her marriage, for emotional health for the children, for financial help, for changes
in her circumstances.

To pray the sorts of thoughts that are on God's mind for
Karen, though, means that I must pray biblically, taking the
vocabulary, the sentences, the concepts in the prayers of Bible
authors, and recycling them for her. It is so easy to pray for
relief without giving much thought to God's purposes; without ever considering his long-range plans for Karen, including her knowledge of God, her likeness to Christ, or the

glory that is being created. Sometimes I "fill in the blank" by putting her name into Ephesians 1:15–19, Philippians 1:9–11, or Colossians 1:9–12, praying for her exactly what Paul asked for his churches. Sometimes prayer is more like a yearning that is hooked up to Romans 8:26–27 where the Spirit intercedes for us according to God's will with groans that words cannot express.

I would like "to make it all better" for Karen, to speed her quickly through the pauses, but I cannot. And if I could, I would fail her by doing so. I know the "must" of suffering, and though I can help in many ways, I must allow her to cultivate hope that is attached to God, not to me. I am quite confident that she is basically preoccupied with God, that her hope and patience originate in sound doctrine, and that she is being strengthened by actual battle. Meeting needs where I can, I still must allow room and time for the growth of patience, character, and the hope of glory, which requires sensitivity that only the Spirit can give me. When is it best to be with her? When is it best to be *silent*? When should I speak? When will my *absence* best serve to turn her directly to God?

Karen, Hildy, and others like them who move while apparently standing still, constitute a modern Hebrews 11 in their walk by faith. We who watch say this to them: You strongly encourage those of us around you. You are human in your hurt, and that helps other hurting people to see you as approachable. Those of us who are privileged to have box seats in your personal grandstand, observe that you do go on from strength to strength, from glory to glory, from impatience to patience, from the immaturity of the raw recruit to the proven mettle of the experienced veteran.

And the God of all grace, who called you to his eternal glory in Christ, after you have suffered a little while, will himself restore you and make you strong, firm, and steadfast.

1 Peter 5:10

F. B. Meyer told Amy Carmichael of how, when he was feeling anything but strong, firm, and steadfast, he was helped. He had found relief by looking to God inwardly and asking for the opposite of the unwanted quality: "Impatience—Thy patience, Lord; Selfishness—Thy unselfishness, Lord; Roughness—Thy gentleness, Lord. . . . Resentment, inward heat, fuss—Thy sweetness, Lord, Thy calmness, Thy peacefulness."[7]

In waiting on God, a lifelong conversation with him emerges as the important element. My awareness of its being a wait in progress reminds me to talk with him. When I am fretful, when I am in turmoil, what quality of his "personality" do he and I need to discuss? What is he like? Who is he? How can I begin to resemble him in this moment? Which of his characteristics could flow toward me, through me, and from me in this particular distress?

For discouragement, give me your courage, Lord. For a full-fledged, demanding urge to quit, give me your perseverance, Lord. Suffering deepens intimacy with God; one's knowledge of him becomes top priority, and nothing can beat this involvement, this partaking of his nature (2 Peter 1:4). My waiting on God means I have found Someone more important than myself, and it means progress.

Perseverance means progress through the earthly wilderness as well as a progressive movement of spirit toward God. Earlier I defined *thlipsis* as pain that results from outward pressure. Scripturally defined patience or perseverance is resistance to that pressure. It is the refusal to give up or to give in. This does *not* mean passively sitting in the desert, waiting to die of thirst. This *does* mean accepting the unchangeable in the landscape and looking for water. Perseverance and acceptance mean resistance to resignation, not passivity, but spiritual activity.

The idea of active patience is found in Romans 8: The creation waits eagerly for the revelation of the sons of God. The term Paul uses for eager waiting conveys to us the tense physical posture of one who is ready to spring out and meet the expected object of desire. Such waiting connects with patience because the glorious end cannot be hurried, yet the waiting is eager, active, and free from other distractions. Although such an intense waiting on the part of creation may be hard to imagine, it is easier to picture the believer straining forward, like a runner ready to take off, waiting eagerly for adoption as God's son (Rom. 8:19, 23). In the waiting process, both creation and the children of God groan.

These groans are like birth pangs. Sustained in hope, they express a deep longing for redemption; they are not the groans expressing pain in the throes of *death*, but the groans that precede *life*. The Spirit inspires in the Christian positive longings and puts him or her on tiptoe in hope. Patience of this variety bears no resemblance to resignation or inertia, and Paul reminds us of it yet again by saying that we hope and wait patiently for "what we do not yet have" (Rom. 8:24–25). We lean expectantly toward what we do not yet have: full freedom of glory as it will one day be revealed, complete adoption and redemption, the full declaration of our sonship. We gain "faith in the Creator's ability, judging by his past performance, to regenerate a tragic world, to come up with one that can feed directly on his own life."[8]

Yes, patience is active and energetic, and it doesn't rub us the wrong way inwardly, as impatience does. Impatience may mean I am still preoccupied with the problem rather than with God. My impatience, once it takes root, grows rapidly. It was at just such a time that I sorted through some old letters where I knew I would find the words of a helpful hymn:

> Not so in haste, my heart!
> Have faith in God and wait;
> Although He linger long,
> He never comes too late.

He never cometh late;
He knoweth what is best;
Vex not thyself in vain;
Until He cometh, rest.

Until He cometh, rest,
Nor grudge the hours that roll;
The feet that wait for God
Are soonest at the goal.

Are soonest at the goal
That is not gained by speed;
Then hold thee still, my heart,
For I shall wait His lead.[9]

Absolutely impossible is the growth of perseverance and a refusal "to grudge the hours" that pass if we are trying to generate growth ourselves! But by the ministry of the Holy Spirit in us, suffering does indeed produce active patience. And this perseverance produces character.

Such patient endurance as faith exhibits under the discipline of tribulation is in its turn the source of [character] . . . the quality of provedness which is possessed by faith when it has stood up to testing, like the precious metal which is left when the base metals have been refined away.[10]

Think about gold refining for a moment. Before one can begin the purifying process that produces gold, massive steel jaws have to shatter tons of rock. After that, the rock undergoes further crushing in huge tumblers where steel balls pulverize it. Following the addition of air and cyanide, the mixture enters tanks for settling and filtration where zinc dust is added to separate the cyanide from the gold. Still impure, the gold is melted with borax, and as it cools, the gold separates from the impurities. This is quite a process—two-and-one-half tons of rock for one ounce of gold![11]

Anyone who has ever suffered can identify with steel jaws and chemicals! According to Peter, our faith is more precious than gold, and our suffering proves that the faith is genuine (1 Peter 1:3–9). The Old Testament uses the same family of words as did Peter to speak of valid currency or genuine coins. Paul also used the same terminology when he wrote of character.

Character is translated in many ways in the English versions of the New Testament: as experience, as proven character, or as a combination—"proof that we have stood the test."[12] That which is "proven" is recognized, approved, or accepted, and is the opposite of that which is shown to be a sham.

Job made a few mistakes, but he proved to be genuine in his faith, not a sham.[13] Before his afflictions came, he had grown spiritually strong by the exercising of spiritual disciplines. Obedience to God was a regular custom for him, and he was ready when calamity struck. Thus, in the middle of his trials, Job was able to say, "when he has tested me, I will come forth as gold" (Job 23:10).

Refining purifies gold. Refining takes time and requires pauses. Refining—suffering—creates patience, and patience produces tested, established character. Consider "what the Lord finally brought about" in Job's life (James 5:11). At long last, God gave Job tangible answers, restoring his impressive wealth of relationships and possessions. But when God first responded to Job's questions, he did not come with easy answers. God comes to us as he came to Job, not *with* the answer, but *as* the answer.

Job replied to God, "my ears had heard of you, but now my eyes have seen you" (Job 42:5). Perhaps Job had slipped into a routine "knowing God," but refining brought him into an exciting phase of discovery.

Probably the highest driving force we have is the need for new experiences, the development of new friendships and vital new relationships. Experiences that once were fresh can become routine; . . . knowledge once exciting becomes routine. God is a God of creativity, and a great need for those of the household of faith is to continue to grow in a creative way.[14]

Nothing works more efficiently or creatively to guarantee growth in my life than does suffering. Hildy would say that. By considering God's character while enduring pain as Job did, you and Hildy and I can, en route to being glorified, begin to participate in his nature.

A friend of mine is an incest survivor. She has struggled through many years of waiting on God, of examining his nature, and has been able to leave behind a large part of the pain, guilt, anger, and feeling of contamination. Because of her suffering, she is a godly woman who bears a closer resemblance to her heavenly Father than to her earthly father. I am also friends with blacks and whites in South Africa, believers who have waited on God every day for years, needing grace from him to live in an unjust society. They have required God's wisdom to know how and when to act. Being in the presence of these South African saints reminds me of God. I think of my friend, an aging widower, who has had both hips replaced by artificial materials, and who now lives with a physical wound that does not heal. He waits for God moment by moment, and in doing so, finds quality in life.

There is an intangible radiance that remains in a room when these people have left it. Suffering produces perseverance; perseverance, character; and character, hope. Not just any hope and not just a hope for relief.

12

Hope, Certain and Solid

"Deann, will I make it?"

"I don't know, Marilyn, but I know you must try." Deann
had earned the nickname Hope after an accident in which
her car was struck by a drunken driver. Marilyn, Deann's
passenger-seat friend, had absorbed most of the impact, and
was given no hope by the medical people who attended her.

Though muddled by medication and weakness, Marilyn
asked Deann to be a coach and inspire her to fight for life.
Deann, at first, flatly refused! With rather typical insight, and
probably some feelings of inadequacy, Deann saw the need
to be a team player with Marilyn—to enlist God as the coach.
There was no doubt about *his* willingness! Marilyn asked
Deann to come up with a team name. The only word that
kept coming to Deann's mind was "hope," and so in the hospital, the "Hope Team" was formed. God as Coach, the two
young women, and the medical group fought, and finally
won. Marilyn lived, but was not expected to walk.

Months of therapy passed, months with the ups and downs that contrasted hope with despair and made the meanings of each word clearer within Marilyn and Deann. During this time, Deann bought two sweatshirts for the team with large letters on the front that spelled HOPE. (I have a rather irreverent mental picture of God on the sidelines also wearing a red sweatshirt with HOPE emblazoned on it.) Finally the day came when the doctor asked Marilyn if she would like to try to walk. The therapist held the protective device that gave Marilyn balance. Biting her lip, gritting her teeth, flexing her muscles, and tensing her will, she tried . . . she walked!

Deann had worn "Hope" on her sweatshirt and in her attitude. She personified hope for Marilyn, and now to many who know her, she is Hope. Every time I use her new name, I experience a little inward leap of joy, like coffee that is percolating.

Now, when I write of hope as a feeling centered in Christ, I think of Hope, the person. Scriptural *hope* is a rich term, filled to capacity like Deann's and Marilyn's histories. Biblical hope almost explodes with exciting truth, more truth than we can easily handle. A study of the vocabulary of hope in the Old Testament is complicated by the fact that in English we tend to think of hope as tied only to future events. But the Old Testament emphasizes that

> hope is not in the first place a situation of tension toward the future—it is above all, a situation of surrender and trust, which . . . cannot be realized in a vacuum but . . . requires one who stands over against us and calls us to trust.[1]

Who stands opposite us across chasms of doubt and calls us to trust? God. He called the people of the Old Testament to trust him, to hope, just as Deann called Marilyn to hope. Distinct from anything secular society describes, hope is not just a consoling dream or herbal drug for pain. Hope becomes someone standing there calling forth positive energy; thus hope becomes a positive emotion within. This kind of hope grew out of Israel's history, out of actual events that had proved God's faithfulness.

Being stretched out toward God, longing after God, waiting for God—just as hope is grammatically attached to God in these lines, it was firmly attached to God in life. Hope is not far removed from the idea of trust. The concepts of safety, security, and reliance on God are found throughout the families of words that we translate *hope*.[2]

Not moving far from hope that connotes the idea of *trust*, we encounter hope that connotes *patience*. A central function in both trust and patience is our waiting for God. There is not only a psychological definiteness, but also a theological definiteness to patience, hope, and trust when the spotlight is on God. "No one whose hope is in you will ever be put to shame," (Ps. 25:3) is a far cry from the fool's hope without God, a hope that comes to nothing (Ps. 14:1; Eph. 2:12). Romans echoes the Psalms, "the one who trusts in him will never be put to shame" (Rom. 9:33).

Romans 5:1–11 and the entire New Testament underline the certainty of our hope, certainty rooted in the cross and the resurrection. What a solid hope! This is nothing at all like our comparatively frivolous use of *hope*, in saying for example, "I hope my team wins the game," or, "I hope the weather soon changes."

In the closing days of 1989, as we watched videotapes of the Berlin wall coming down, and people rising up whose dreams had been stifled for decades, newscasters searched their vocabularies for synonyms for hope. Reporters stood before us on television with pieces of rock in their hands, and we all sat amazed that bits of an old wall could fascinate us so. Atop what now remained of the wall, in sight of newly broken-through gates, Berliners laughed and cried and sang. They personified hope, and we wept with joy for them.

Still we wait expectantly to see what the rapid changes in Eastern Europe will bring. Can permanent change actually occur quickly? Will new governments embrace democracy as we think of it? Our hopes are real, but tentative. Our expectations are high, but if we are honest, we admit our hopes are weakened with doubtful questions: "Can it really be?" Waiting to see, the world heartily hopes that true peace and unity break out and continue.

But biblical hope is *not* a synonym for hearty hope, or "wishing hard." It is far more solid than our most respectable or noble earthly hopes, and it is not streaked with doubt.

Biblical hope *cannot* disappoint us because God expresses his love for us in Christ's death and by His Spirit (Rom. 5:5–8). Such hope is stable because it is not grounded in fluctuating and uncertain circumstances, nor is it related to changing moods. Such hope is rooted deeply in the unshakable, undeviating sureness of God's character. We once again run into the urgency of acquiring a deep knowledge of God's character! How else can we know the solidity of biblical hope that is a direct extension of who God is?

This sort of hope is more than a "believing posture," more than a positive emotion, more than a good feeling about the future. Far more than merely a clean-burning fuel for our motivations, *Christ* is "the hope of glory." Men and women without Christ are "without hope and without God." Paul wrote to Timothy by the command of God and "Christ Jesus our Hope." He spoke of "endurance inspired by hope in our Lord Jesus Christ." We may honestly say that our hope is centered on everlasting life, salvation, redemption, righteousness, and the resurrection, each of which leads directly back to Christ himself as Source, as Author, and as Finisher.[3]

As the *object* of my hope, Jesus Christ inevitably affects my thoughts and creates an *attitude* of hope, just as he did for Marilyn after her accident.

When a shipwrecked sailor . . . knows that "this boat is my hope," the hope is fixed on the approaching instrument of salvation. He identifies that which exists outside himself as his hope.[4]

The Wreck of the Hesperus, a poem my dad taught me when I was in elementary school, tells of a captain who took his daughter with him to sea, where their ship crashed during a violent hurricane. As a child I was always moved by the hopelessness of their situation. The young girl saw lights and hoped these were at the prow of a rescue boat, but the lights must have been on a faraway coast. She heard sounds that she thought were guns, and her father said that the noise came from another ship in distress. She heard "church bells" that were really foghorns. No rescue; no fixed hope; they drowned, and the poem ends with a prayer for us who read their story.[5]

A storm-tossed sailor, Peter learned quickly enough that Christ, as the "approaching instrument of salvation," was his hope. His keeping his eyes fixed on Christ obviously affected not only his attitude but also how much water he swallowed! Water was not compatible with life, and hope became a practical necessity. Christ was Peter's hope, and hope characterized Peter's attitude.

In Scripture, hope moves between these two ideas: hope as an attitude, and Christ's approaching us as our hope. Having described hardships and great pressure to the point of despairing of life, Paul says these things happened to teach him to rely not on himself, but on God: "On Him we have set our hope" (2 Cor. 1:10).

Setting our hope on Christ is not religious wishful thinking, not a kind of pious fiction, not an unrealistic fantasy, not an opiate for contemporary headaches. Biblical hope is entirely realistic. It wrestles with the worst that comes, and can be called realistic because it takes seriously every tragedy that is a part of reality. In Romans 1–3, the reality of sin is bluntly described, and there is bleak hopelessness; but once Paul turns to justification through faith in Christ, he writes "the hope of glory," a phrase that extends beyond our ability to comprehend. He tells us that creation was subjected to frustration in the certain hope of its being liberated into the freedom of glory. We as Christians *live* a hope that contradicts the realities of this world—a hope that contradicts sin and frustration, a hope that is fed by our faith in God's faithfulness.

Patience and hope, defined biblically, include trust. Earlier we studied another term that was lined with trust: *rejoicing*. Hope, when it swells almost to the bursting point, becomes rejoicing. It is as if, looking at hope from one angle, we see it as patient endurance, but scrutinizing it from another angle, we see it as sure confidence wherein the hopeful person pirouettes right out into rejoicing.

Think again about suffering, rejoicing, patience, character, and hope. "It is in the hour of . . . suffering that the longing for union with *God* makes itself felt."[6] It is both in and after the hour of most difficult struggle that we learn to rejoice or boast in *God*. Patience is an active waiting on whom? *God*. Our own character changes as we interact with *God's* character. Hope has *God* as its focus.

Paul ties the whole discussion of hope to God. If God is who he claims to be in Scripture (and he is), if the truth as truth is unchanging (and it is), then will suffering *always* create patience, character, and hope? No.

Rhythm for Choice

[Suffering causes a person] to decide which
position he will take up, for or against God.

Josef Scharbert

You must realize from the outset that the goal
towards which He is beginning to guide you is
absolute perfection, and no power in the whole
universe, except you yourself, can prevent Him
from taking you to that goal. . . . To shrink back
from that plan is not humility; it is laziness or
cowardice. To submit to it is not conceit or
megalomania; it is obedience.

C. S. Lewis

13

The Crux of the Matter

"No, hope didn't just drop into my lap," Ruth confessed. "Feeling the sharpness of grief, I knew I had some conscious choices to make. The experience of walking with God in the previous years was a strong foundation, but these situations presented fresh choices." Ruth was dealing with grief. Her husband had suddenly died and then twin granddaughters arrived, Nora and Meg. Soon word came that Nora was a dwarf; she would never grow normally.

Yet the truth of God's faithfulness punctuates Ruth's life, in these life-halting pauses as well as in her gradual adjustment to slow-paced glaucoma. The death of her husband of forty years; twin grandchildren, one with a great disability; three sons living far from her (in Germany, the United States, and Canada); failing vision; giving up her car and no longer driving; and selling her home in Illinois to enter a retirement center have been other adjustments she has had to make, all within ten years.

With hard-won peace based on hard choices, Ruth affirms that God is faithful and good. Ruth's friends are warmed by her joy, which has matured in these years. Conscious decisions to cooperate with the Spirit, to know Christ and the power of his resurrection *and* the fellowship of his suffering, to accept God's allowing Nora to enter life as a dwarf, to accept that God is permitting her vision to fail, and to accept that he took her husband when they had followed all the rules to prevent further heart attacks are all choices that have brought peace.

These were hard choices. But *choice* and *decision* mean that refusal was possible.

If you're like me, you'd rather not think about making hard choices. At this stage, you may want to rush ahead to study the chapters on rejoicing and glorying.

This urge to move on reminds me of my trying to drive a car with an automatic transmission after years of driving with a standard transmission. After futilely trying to move the car, I realized that the strange rocking motion, forward and backward, was the result of my having one foot on the brake, as if it were a clutch, and the other on the gas. Margi, my good, laugh-ready friend, was with me; we laughed so hard that I know I will never live it down.

In the matters of suffering and choice some will step on the accelerator, and others will hit the brake. The confusion of both will plague still others. But eventually a clear choice can be made because suffering will cause a person to decide the position he will take—for God or against him. We are free to refuse God and his plans, his ways.

We will not receive warnings as we do when the radio announcer says, "This is a test. I repeat, this is a test. In the event of a crisis, you will hear this sound. . . ." Different crises will come into life, unannounced; each is either an opportunity to decide for God or a temptation to decide against him. Choosing to trust God and go on with him will mean my "wrestling, [my] stretching out with every effort of the soul," inspired by Christ who suffered and by the Spirit who generates hope.[1]

I remember the first time I heard the traffic reporter say that the Edens Expressway near Chicago was a "long, thin parking lot." It was easy to chuckle at such a humorous and accurate expression as I drove along my traffic-free suburban street. But it probably was not funny to the folks "parked" on that freeway, and it definitely is not funny when Christians are similarly stuck because one foot is on the brake while the other is on the accelerator. When the car danced awkwardly back and forth that evening in Ruth's driveway, I had chosen both pedals. Before I could progress, I had to consciously choose the accelerator. What about believers' choices in that long, thin, parking lot where they stall, not progressing from suffering to patience to tested character to hope as Ruth has?

I think of a divorcee who, after years of stop-and-go, and fueled by bitterness instead of the Spirit's energy, has moved perhaps an inch, forgiving neither God nor her former husband. I think of another person who stays in a marriage, but only appears to do so, having emotionally departed long ago. I think of a woman who struggles with the fact of singleness, and seems to do so without evident progress. Check the other traffic lanes. A woman is passing who was once a victim of divorce, but is no longer. Great hurt and difficulty accompanied her divorce, but a survivor's steady movement that defies natural explanation, a gradual healing that amazes friends, a new gentleness of spirit that attracts others, and symptoms of young joy that baffle the distant spectator have taken over. I actually know such a woman. In that other lane, a married couple drives along; he stays, and I mean *stays with* and works at their marriage though leaving would have been so very easy. I know such a man. There goes a van, filled with friends traveling with the single woman at the wheel. She is pursuing God, growing as a person, developing significant friendships; yes, hurting sometimes and admitting it to

trusted friends, but consciously choosing and reevaluating
her mind-set. Yes, I know such a woman.

What is the difference between the folks who might as well
be in "park," and the latter group who are in "drive"? Some
respond to buried choices that have not received sufficient
conscious thought. Some chose to set their "brakes," determined to remain "parking lot residents." My criticizing them
could be unwise, partly because of their individual and unknown differences, but also because I tend to "drive" with
one foot on the brake when I am in or emerging from pain.

Many folks in the jammed parking lot of life live with a
semblance, a pretense of truth. For spiritual well-being they
need to gain an *awareness* of choices they have made, but ig-
nored. Some are not actually convinced "way down deep"
that God, using the extremely raw material of suffering, can
create patience, character, and the hope of glory. They choose
not to own the truth, even though they may read it and hear
it preached.

Others have become too comfortable in a stationary
position. They choose not to examine and know the truth.
Still others have sat still long enough to be in a daze, and they
don't acknowledge that they are choosing at all. They select
immobility—choosing a lie that says God doesn't do what
he promises, or mean what he says.

Choice—by now you may have scanned Romans 5 wondering where *choice* is written in the text. It stands behind
the passage and is hidden in the word, *know*: "We also rejoice in our sufferings, because we know. . . ." We must understand our *knowing* and what it means to *know* the specific truth of Romans, chapters 5 and 8.

Paul used this particular term, *know*, when he was speaking of well-known or generally accepted *facts*—positively
certain facts based on experience. In his letters, this is knowledge connected with faith, knowledge that is absolutely valid.[2]
There is an important element of knowledge in Paul's idea
of faith; faith rests on a knowing, and from this knowing,

faith receives its strength. Knowledge and faith fill up or complete one other, each requiring the other to make a whole package, a full definition. If we could fly brightly colored flags from every faith promise in Romans, the book would be very eye-catching. Those who choose "life" are justified by *faith*. And those justified by *faith* have peace with God and arrive at rejoicing because of something they *know* (Rom. 1:17; 5:1; 5:3–4).

The act of choosing God in the middle of suffering isn't thoughtless. Sparks seem to fly back and forth between the realities of suffering and hope in our lives, not harmfully explosive sparks, not electrically shocking sparks, but flashes of vitality that catch our attention.[3] Once God has gained our attention, he intrigues us with the active verb "produces." Suffering produces.

Pain, though, doesn't produce quickly. Certain hurts don't get healed as rapidly as do others. Suffering has no money-back guarantee: "refundable if not productive in three days." Resurrection life may take longer than three days to surface, but when we follow God's instructions, suffering will eventually, and certainly, produce. Suffering produces, brings about, accomplishes, achieves, and creates. "Our light and momentary troubles *are creating* for us an eternal glory that far outweighs them all" (2 Cor. 4:17, my paraphrase).

Creates is an intense word. The hope and glory that result are *not* mere compensations for what we've gone through; they are not accidental results, not by-products, not incidentals. Our suffering actually *creates* the hope of glory, *creates* the glory itself.

The Holy Spirit is the source of this productive creativity. His calendar covers each person's lifetime (Rom. 15:13), "And we, who with unveiled faces all reflect the Lord's glory, are being transformed into his likeness with ever-increasing glory, which comes from the Lord, who is the Spirit" (2 Cor. 3:18). In spite of severe suffering, the Thessalonians exhibited joy, joy given by the Spirit (1 Thess. 1:6). In spite of my friend Ruth's suffering, she is joyous.

Will suffering invariably produce the positives that Paul lists or the joy that Ruth has? Is the ascent to hope automatic—the Christian + suffering + the Spirit = hope and joy? As we look around us at people who hurt we agree that suffering will produce *something*. Martin Luther wrote that for those who do not know God, tribulation works impatience and despair, among other things; we each know believers and unbelievers who are indistinguishable under stress.[4]

Countless people have survived rejection or other kinds of trauma, but have not moved on to inward healing. These are bitter, hurt, withdrawn, or withdrawing people, who shout or whisper or cry, "Never, never again will I trust. I've had enough! Enough!" We know many, who like Naomi, want to change their names from meaning pleasant, to Mara, which means bitter. Although Naomi never did actually make that change (Ruth 1:20–21) we know many, Christian and non-Christian, who succeed all too well.

Look at Romans 8:28 again, "for those who love God, who have been called according to his purpose, all things work together for good" (my paraphrase). For those who love God, not with a sentimental, sticky, or saccharine "love," but who are learning to love with his covenant love, to love with his same committed-for-all-time-and-eternity love, "for those called according to his purpose," all things work together for good. This was true for Naomi, Job, and Paul. For twentieth-century believers like Ric in his developmental disablement, for Ric's family, for Ruth, for Nora, and for those believers whose names we want to fill in here, all things work together for good.[5]

Can we fill in any Christian's name? No. We cannot write in another's name because the ascent up this ladder of patience, character, and hope demands a choice, an individual choice that one person cannot make for another. Because of a conscious choice to cooperate with God's grace, Martha, Ric's mother, is able to write, "I am closer to God because of Ric."[6] Ruth will tell you she is closer to God because of Nora. Both women are learning patience; building character; gaining hope, the hope of glory; knowing God now, and knowing a taste of glory yet to come.

While Ruth's and Martha's present difficulties are not the result of the sins of others, Angie, a friend of mine, is choosing to work at overcoming the results of sexual abuse, the sin of her mother.

"Powerless. Hopeless. Afraid. As a five-year-old, and again last summer when the memories began to surface, I felt just that—powerless, hopeless, and afraid." Memories of shameful abuse, repressed, pushed under, locked up, frozen for thirty-five years surfaced, but Angie has found the power, hope, and courage that are necessary to change the chaotic pandemonium of inner emotions—God's power, hope, and courage. She says that before she came to Christ her inner self felt like an orchestra that never finished tuning up; having now spent years with him, she makes music I love to hear.

For Angie, real change meant making the difficult choice to examine her history and create a better future. She has grown tremendously in the twelve years I've known her. The key to her growth has been her consistent, positive choices. These days, while she has to put on the brake if memories come too fast, she maintains steady movement forward.

Because Angie feeds on Scripture her knowledge of God increases and her faith grows. She exercises her faith, and her faith matures, which develops knowledge of God and his truth, and its application in life. She no longer muddles along with her heart and mind incommunicado, the one out of contact with the other so that knowledge and faith are separated. Rather, for Angie, knowledge and faith inform and support one another.

Quite a dialogue between knowledge and faith wrestled inside the writer of Psalm 73. Asaph lived for a while with the illusion that God was not treating him well enough—a familiar scene in our own skirmishes with God. His confusion, though, was canceled when he entered God's presence. He had been worried about the prosperity of those who did not follow God, and wrote, "When I tried to understand . . . it was oppressive, until I entered the sanctuary of God; then I understood. . . ." What beautiful truth depends on that little word, *until*! This is an example of the Old Testament view that knowledge is the result of a personal encounter; Asaph's knowledge and faith affected each other as he *chose* to encounter God in worship.[7]

Like Asaph, we choose whether we will feed our knowledge and whether we will exercise faith. Like the homesick man in Psalm 84, we decide, by faith, to set our hearts on the pilgrimage that, though perhaps winding through the "Valley of Weeping," leads home. By the means of knowledge and faith we make such a valley into a place of springs.[8] We choose what to believe. We choose whether to believe truly and deeply that which we say we believe. We choose whether to *own* knowledge and faith. We choose the kind of prosperity to seek—internal or external.

A believer at times may doubt certain aspects of God's truth. How do I know? Because, true to Scripture's picture of me, I have often sinned by doubting, by refusing to believe God. I have "unbelieved" sections of valid truth. Oh, yes, justification by faith, peace with God, access by faith into grace—we'll choose that. We have accepted Romans 5:1–2. What about owning verses three and four—rejoicing in our suffering?

The largest expense for some will be in giving up the untruths they've chosen along the way, like, "I can't change," or "I have a right to be upset about . . . " as well as statements that begin with "But I can't, . . ." meaning, "But I won't . . . " The cost for someone else may be in relinquishing his or her unforgiving attitude when he or she realizes that, as a Christian pardoned so mercifully by God, one can hardly go on and on *and on* refusing to forgive others. We must uproot bitterness before knowledge and faith can thrive.[9]

To give up long held possessions such as unforgiveness and bitterness may require a surprisingly vigorous wrenching (a bit like a dental extraction), but the exchange of decay for health, the exchange of lies for truth, is performed because of an inward choice, facilitated by the Holy Spirit. Although it may be initially difficult, it is unfailingly wise and indescribably rewarding to choose that which is right.

Virginia Stem Owens, in her description of enjoying a snowstorm on the Wind River in Wyoming, moves us to make pricey choices. Of the perfect calligraphy written in snow in the canyon, she says,

> this particular hieroglyph for "beautiful" has a price. It is not come by easily. No one, of course, insists you buy. The world is not hawking its wares. . . . Stay inside by the fire. It doesn't care. It will keep this word to itself as readily as not, hidden from stove-warmed hands and feet.[10]

The choices we are considering in Romans seem to demand great personal cost, but these reluctant and difficult experiences of obedience bring their own kind of reward, a reward more valuable than the easier, less-struggled-with obediences.

Love for our Lord always means obedience; obedience may mean sacrifice; in this context it means giving up our bitterness. While sacrifice inevitably means pain, obedience and sacrifice ultimately yield joy. Because of Christ, sacrifice brings spiritual liveliness beyond death to self. Angie lives this concept.

Bitterness, unforgiveness, a refusal to accept the truth—all these are barriers wedged between the text and our daily lives. They act as obstacles to our intimately knowing God and to ultimate joy, hope, and glory. These hindrances to our

deep and lived-out knowledge of truth must be faced, so that
we do not, in the dailiness of the Christian walk, continue
mentally to leapfrog over the choices we make *emotionally*.
Our knowing that suffering creates numerous positives must
become a deep knowing, agreeing, by conscious choice, with
God.

No power in the universe can block the truth from setting
a person free, except the individual who refuses to know it,
to accept it, or to own it in mind and heart. "If you hold to
my teaching, you are really my disciples. Then you will know
the truth, and the truth will set you free."[11] *If, . . . then. . . .*

Will it be the gas pedal or the brake? The parking lot or
the thruway?

I cannot ask those questions without recalling a situation
I described to you earlier: the occasion when "my" family
moved away, with misunderstanding, without healthy closure, and most painfully, without me. My choices made all
the difference to my healing. In this case, it was my refusal
to forgive that added a lead weight to my foot against the
brake. It was necessary for me to give a great deal of conscious thought to whether I wanted to acknowledge Romans
5:3 and 4 as true, whether I wanted to allow the Spirit to
work the text out in my life, whether I was willing to obey
other scriptural truth so that this section of the Bible could
begin to pulsate for, in, and around me.

My thoughts were like heavy pieces of furniture. This old-
fashioned furniture made apparently permanent dents in the
carpet, and my pushing it aside even a few inches showed
that the pile might never stand up again. Besides that, the
furniture was overstuffed and awkward, its corners bruising
me when I tried to move it. I could have stored these thoughts
of unforgiveness for years until they solidified into bitterness,
but I found that they were actually portable, removable.

My problem was not in mentally grasping Paul's words on
suffering and hope; my problem was at the level of my own
will. The journal I kept at that time became important for

processing my thoughts as I took retreats to sort things out. It reveals that my choice to forgive was made five months before *I felt* like forgiving. It took that long for my emotions to catch up with my choice! I am not particularly proud of the delay, but it does illustrate an important fact: The emotions finally follow the path selected by the will and mind. I saw that I could choose to own a number of truths, choosing in the deep underground citadel of my will.[12]

Once that stronghold was affected, my emotions didn't stand a chance, though, of course, they gave strong resistance. Emotions require processing time, and I could allow myself that time of slow healing once I had my direction set. I could then face the massive loss because my struggle was with grief and not with forgiveness. I could finally face the fact that I resented my own need of them, more than I resented them. My grief began to subside. God met my needs. I began to *know* the truth. . . .

Both David and Paul learned these lessons. David poured his heart out before it stopped aching, and leads us through his processing of emotions, thoughts, and choices. He begins several psalms with the problem very much in focus, but his thinking advances until God is central. "What matters is that God, rather than the enemy, fills the foreground before David's eyes."[13]

Like David, if a problem replaced God in the foreground for a while, Paul chose to look beyond it. "We fix our eyes not on what is seen, but on what is unseen. For what is seen is temporary, but what is unseen is eternal." And when did he pen this? Immediately following his comment that light and momentary afflictions are achieving for us a glory that far outweigh our troubles (2 Cor. 4:17–18).

Paul refreshingly admitted to being hard pressed, perplexed, persecuted, and struck down (2 Cor. 4:8–9). We don't often think of Paul as being bewildered or struck down. David poured out his breaking heart for us, often telling us what it was like before his heart mended and he was able to praise. It isn't sub-Christian for tear glands, created by God, to function, but as we follow David's example, if we persist, we end up eventually putting emotion in its place and elevating God to his. Look in the Psalms and, matching David's emotions with yours, pray through the appropriate Psalm as he did.

We need not worry that borrowing the Psalms to process our own feelings is some kind of spiritual plagiarism. Such prayers, in fact, help fulfill the mission of the Psalms—helping us respond to God, serving as guides for answering God's initiative. Eugene Peterson writes convincingly that praying through the Psalms rescues us from the *tyranny* of emotion. Because feelings are

> so emphatically *there* and so incontrovertibly *interior*, . . . we take [them] seriously as reputable guides to the reality that is deep within us—our hearts before God. But feelings are no more spiritual than muscles.[14]

David recognizes, labels, feels, admits, and affirms his emotions, but he always moves beyond them, overcoming their tyranny.

This morning I phoned a friend whom I have not seen for many years and discovered that what I'd heard was true: Her husband had died not long ago. She told me of special comfort God had given one morning when she had been crying. I was saddened at her loss, but delighted that she was able to admit to grief and to tears. So did David, even while he was choosing growth.

So did Paul, and he gave us that lovely picture of the treasure in earthen vessels. Earthen vessels can remain earthen. What a relief! The treasure within us will be all the more apparent in contrast to our earthenness. "Light is a clearer contrast through my cracks and flame is cleaner seen if its container does not compete."[15] Second Corinthians stresses the fact that the death and the life of Jesus were simultaneously evident in the apostle's experience. . . . It was not a matter of life after death, or even life through death, but of life in the midst of death.[16]

Ten years ago I was in a situation where my earthenness seemed all too clear. As I finished my second missionary term in South Africa, the day came when some highly valued friends were to depart for the United States (the friends who received the bookends mentioned previously). I went to the school that morning, and as usual, asked my nursing students to choose a hymn to begin the class. One of them requested "I Surrender All." Realizing that I could not focus on the music through tears, and I had to be able to see to play the accompaniment, I asked them to pick another song. Afterward we had a good talk about whether it is possible to mean the words "I surrender all," and yet cry at the very same time. Yes, it *is* possible. With the will I surrender; I choose God's way, and wait for the emotions to catch up.

Crux comes from the Latin word for *cross*. In English we use this word to speak of a crossroads, the decisive point, the vital center. Will your suffering create hope? Will you allow it to? The crux is a choice, your choice.

Rhythms
for Festival

God has and is a glory . . . [that] awakens joy.

Karl Barth

By "the glory of God" is meant [in Romans five and eight] that illumination of man's whole being by the radiance of the divine glory which is man's true destiny but which was lost through sin, as it will be restored (not just as it was, but immeasurably enriched through God's own personal participation in man's humanity in Jesus Christ). . . .

C. E. B. Cranfield

To please God . . . to be a real ingredient in the divine happiness . . . to be loved by God, not merely pitied, but delighted in as an artist delights in his work or a father in a son—it seems impossible, a weight or burden of glory which our thoughts can hardly sustain. But so it is.

C. S. Lewis

14

My Teardrops Dance

I recall that there were three hard exercises to practice—choosing to own the truth of Romans 5, choosing to forgive, and deciding to apply my understanding of how to "rejoice in suffering." During one of my personal retreats after my adopted family left, I began my five-month trek through emotion. I decided that to live out Romans 5 and to forgive were my only live options; that rejoicing in the middle of distress was an urgent imperative. How? It was not easy, but wading through a knee-deep stream is one thing; wading through a flood that causes ripples and rings around one's neck is another! In those days, Joan, my friend and housemate, kept a box of tissues in every room for regular moppings-up.

Something in me said there was no beauty left, and since I could not tolerate that possibility, part of my self-imposed treatment was to look purposefully for beauty around me. Part of the beauty treatment included observing nature with the change from summer to autumn to winter; writing down the sights, smells, and sounds that pulled me into life (squirrels and birds, Lake Michigan lapping the shore, flowers with soft color and aroma); browsing in gift shops and roaming through metropolitan art galleries each Saturday; and scrutinizing people with the hope of seeing Christ in their clean, clear spirits. There was beauty galore!

Someplace between the park and a gift shop, it occurred to me that it might help to have a tangible reminder of the truth I was incubating. I found just the thing. A small, flat silhouette of a bell hanging on a nearly invisible thread. The bell's center was cut away and contained a crystal teardrop. The crystal tear, to me, meant turmoil; the bell, a reminder of rejoicing and hope though its heart was cut away. It hung on a just-barely-perceptible thread like the truth that seemed thin, transparent, and insubstantial at times.

This little joy bell rang at the right moments—when I was tempted to go back on my choice and "unforgive"; when I glanced at it glimmering just inside my window and stopped to reflect on what it meant to rejoice; and when I became weary in the middle of appointments and could see it as a small reminder of large truth, a reminder that I could physically touch. Actually touching it made pinpoints of light dance on my desk. Have you ever watched a teardrop of truth dancing?

Paul's truth dances. A humanly earthen and sometimes baffled Paul wrote Second Corinthians echoing the facts we find written in Romans 5 and 8. The early emphasis of Second Corinthians is "comfort in the midst of affliction" with a distinctive attitude of "I will rejoice." The main theme toward the end of the book is "strength in the midst of weakness" with an underlying spirit of joy.[1]

Does this mean that I *must* rejoice?

Is there ever a time to persist in saying, "I cannot rejoice"? In one sense, yes, because we *cannot* rejoice; *left to ourselves*, we simply cannot. We have already seen that the Holy Spirit is the source of hope; a part of the fruit of the Spirit is joy, and there is a healthy realization that *on my own*, I cannot rejoice in suffering. Only by the energizing of the Spirit, can I exult. But still. . . .

Must I rejoice? A swarm of reactions buzz around this question. We can avoid being stung if we define the term, *rejoice*. Is there more to rejoicing than the joy aspect? What does it mean to rejoice in suffering after surgery, after being "released" from a job one loves, or after divorce?

Think of faith as a backup system supporting all other components of life. In the New Testament, throughout Romans, and throughout the Christian walk, faith is central, foundational, vital, essential, and urgent. Faith is constantly applied and reapplied.

In those hours when pain is assaulting us, when our emotions are at war with the idea of rejoicing, or when we are too numb even to consider an active word like rejoice, it is time to say, "But I trust. I choose to believe that God is what he says he is, that he does not break promises, that he is unfailingly good, that his ways are absolutely perfect." Knowledge and faith will be engaged in a deep and heavy dialogue, a debate painful in itself; human logic and illogic along with emotion will take well-aimed potshots at the will.

I do not rejoice at the news of a friend's impending mastectomy, nor do I ask her to do so on the day she signs the surgical consent. But I pray for her, asking for what a person cannot have apart from God's giving: grace to trust that God knows her body, her husband, and their lives together. Grace to go on believing that God is good and that he is powerful. And even then, I will not overdo it by heaping coals of spiritual truth on her head through prayer.

By today, as I write about Beth, her breast surgery is past, and she has had months to reflect. At a women's luncheon, she vulnerably told us of her pilgrimage, of her deep-driven trust of God, of her new appreciation of his nature in her pain. Afraid that she spoke too soon after the operation and that she would not be able to mask her emotion, she modeled transparency, being "real," and being faithful to God before the grief had passed. She cried real tears and voiced sincere faith all at the same time.

In the varied arenas of trust in my life, my friends get the credit for listening to me through my tears; Beth says the same, and the Spirit has honored our wilted, weary, wet, but eventual choices to trust. And when I cannot rejoice, but can choose to trust even a little, then that tiny, perhaps microscopic, trust is a movement of obedience. Obedience breeds joy, often to my moist surprise.

Packer dignifies this arguing and reasoning with oneself by calling it "meditation," and I am grateful to him for that.

> Meditation is the activity of calling to mind, and thinking over, and dwelling on, and applying to oneself, the various things that one knows about the works and ways and purposes and promises of God . . . to clear one's mental and spiritual vision of God, and to let His truth make its full and proper impact on one's mind and heart. . . . It is . . . arguing with oneself, reasoning oneself out of moods of doubt and unbelief into a clear apprehension of God's power and grace.[2]

And now we are back to choosing. Will I choose to know, to own the truth, to trust and believe God, to reason and argue with my emotions, to . . . rejoice? "Well," you say, "perhaps, but wait a minute, read me the fine print . . . what exactly did Paul mean by *rejoice*?"

Perhaps you picture rejoicing as a merry jig or dance in the streets, an unrestrained burst of laughter, a deeply felt smile accompanied by twinkling eyes, or a very pleasant and healthy "heart condition." When we encounter it, we soon become curious about the stimulus for such exultation. What has triggered it? Many years ago a stranger on a bus asked me why I was so happy. I wondered how she knew I was happy, and replied by asking her what gave me away. She said I had been singing ever since I had sat down!

So now you are as curious as she. Shall I tell you why I was forcing a solo on an unknown public? I was in Durban, South Africa, en route to meet friends, and I must confess to singing the doxology and other songs of thanksgiving all the way to the airport. The objects of my rejoicing were two friends, Mary and Stan. The focus of my rejoicing was fully as significant as the verb itself.

Long before its use in Romans 5, *I rejoice*, and its synonym, *I boast*, meant to plume oneself. I think of a long, soft, fluffy, ostrich feather, tucked quite conspicuously in the hat of a proud person preening herself before a mirror. Or I think of a peacock strutting about in multicolored, satin glory, its chest swollen with self-importance, its feathers spread in a self-aware display. Or sometimes, I think of a camel looking down his nose as only supercilious camels can do, haughty disdain in every condescending expression. We are perhaps more patient when it comes to the preening of birds and animals, but we want to turn away from preening people. Like us, the ancient Greeks had no room for the arrogant person who enjoyed loudly trumpeting his own strengths and honors.

Our reaction to boasting, when the object of boasting is self, is much the same as was the Greeks'. This sort of boasting is not merely a casual fault; it is seen in Scripture as foolish. Preening, strutting, blowing one's own horn, a glance sliding down the nose and falling objectionably off the end— all of these are socially and spiritually unacceptable. Paul used this word, *boasting*, to teach us that sin consists of glorifying ourselves and not giving God the honor he deserves.

"Sin . . . is self-coronation."[3] Our natural impulses will lead us to organize grand coronations at every turn. I crown thee, "Queen Me." Bring on the ermine, hand me the scepter, and polish the crown! The self will characteristically glory in itself, trust in itself, and primp emotionally with every available listener, but Paul was out to tell us about a healthy, attractive, and *true* boast, humbling oneself before God, boasting or glorying in him.

He used the term in writing of the Jews' boasting in the law and their bragging about their closeness to God. He also used it in warning the Corinthians not to continue boasting about God's human instruments, their teachers. He describes Christians as those who glory or boast in Christ; he describes the enemies of the cross as those whose glory was their own shame.[4] The Old Testament warns, "One who puts on his armor should not boast like one who takes it off" (1 Kings 20:11). And in Psalm 49:6 we are advised against boasting in great riches.

In giving the term *boast* or *rejoice* its New Testament meaning, Paul was echoing the Old Testament wherein *trust* was a primary component of the word. "What is most deeply at stake in the concept 'boasting' is the question as to what it is in which man places his trust."[5] Should the Jews trust in the law and their own ability to keep it? Should believers trust their teachers ahead of God? Should a soldier trust the power represented in his armor? Should the wealthy put confidence in their money?

A generous amount of the ingredient called trust gives a whole new flavor to the idea of rejoicing. As we might expect, this boasting, this rejoicing does carry delight and thanksgiving in its definition. Yes, there is the sense of "taking joy in" or "glorying in" a person, a circumstance, an idea, or an object, but we must do as Paul did, and pack this word with scriptural meaning.

Biblical rejoicing carries with it the quietness and confidence of relying on, resting in, or trusting. It includes the merry dance, the deeply felt smile, and the twinkling eyes, but *first* it includes the believing heart, the bowed head, and open hands stretched out in faith, confident of God's response. Waiting in a trust-poised posture precedes the finale of a small leap of joy.

This concept of rejoicing that has been blended with trust becomes clearer when we look at the opposite of rejoicing or boasting. Particularly in the Old Testament, the opposite of rejoicing is to be "put to shame," or to be disappointed, confounded, or disillusioned (Jer. 2:36; Isa. 28:16; Rom. 9:33). If rejoicing is focused on an inappropriate or unworthy object, for example, armor with its inevitable chinks, negative results are fully guaranteed.

But those who trust—with God as the object of trust—those who continue to trust are *not* disappointed. They cannot be disillusioned because they have no illusions to begin with if their trust is in God and not in a temporal or earthly substitute. They cannot be put to shame or confounded because God is the stimulus and focus for their faith, hope, and joy. When Romans 5:1–5 climaxes, it is with hope that "does not disappoint us, because God has poured out his love." The firmness of the words, *does not disappoint,* is totally certain and solid because it is rooted in the historical events of the cross and resurrection. In what should we rejoice, exult, or trust? On what can we rely and rest? The answer comes with clarity.

There is only one legitimate boast, one correct focus for rejoicing, one in whom we can truly exult and trust, one on whom we can rely: God. This truth lies at the heart of Romans 5:1–11, and influences our every step on the way toward understanding the passage. Our rejoicing in the hope of glory (v. 2) would be abysmally empty apart from rejoicing in God (v. 11).

"But," you ask, "didn't Rev. Mac's hope turn out to be abysmally empty in his suicide?" What about this Christian man who finished his earthly life himself? Wasn't that a hopeless, empty boast?" If he could speak from heaven, he might say, "Yes, I felt all of that. But my true hope was rooted in the cross and resurrection. My death was not ultimately hopeless. Christ has not disappointed me."

There is one basic boast, one becoming boast, one right rejoicing. Paul more than once quotes Jeremiah, a man who had considerable expertise in suffering.

> "Let not the wise man boast of his wisdom
>   or the strong man boast of his strength
>   or the rich man boast of his riches,
> but let him who boasts boast about this:
>   that he understands and knows me,
> that I am the LORD, who exercises kindness,
>   justice, and righteousness on the earth,
>   for in these I delight," declares the LORD.
>   Jeremiah 9:23–24

What do you boast or glory in? During my debut as a traveling vocalist on that bus, I was glorying in my friends and their imminent arrival. Not so long ago I watched a four-year-old leap six inches off the carpet as she rejoiced in the prospect of being a flower girl, in her mind, "a princess." We associate such exuberance with childlikeness: granddaughters wanting to somersault down the steps as Grandma arrives, or the child in me, clapping her hands as a car, bringing a significant someone, turns in the driveway. The little granddaughters or the fifty-two-year-old me have one thing in common, we know, and in some measure we understand, the object of our rejoicing. I admit to glorying in, rejoicing in, and fully trusting this man whom I am privileged to call husband. I know and understand him, and that knowledge is a requirement in order for the rejoicing to occur and to be valid.

God says, "But let not those who are married, boast primarily in their marriage; nor let those who are friends, boast above all in their friendships; nor let the faithful rejoice in their own ability to walk with Me; these are given as expressions of My lovingkindness, justice, righteousness and delight. Let them rejoice dancingly in this: that they understand and know Me" (Jer. 9:23–24 adapted).

15

Rejoicing in Suffering

"Of course, it's not that I rejoice because I came from a dysfunctional family. No way! But I rejoice in what God has done in spite of it. And even in his using it to make me who I am." Danette displays New Testament living. She has grasped what Paul, Peter, and James tell us. The adult child of alcoholic parents and the product of a family that functioned abnormally, Danette has known Christ for only a few years. During her junior year in college, her father suddenly died; she reeled. Christian friends, who were closer to her than I, offered supporting hands until she regained her equilibrium. Then in her senior year, a truck collided with her mother's car, throwing her mom into a permanent childish simplicity. Now acting as her mother's parent, Danette at age twenty-five is about forty-five in certain areas of maturity.

She would never suggest rejoicing in alcoholism, a dysfunctioning family, a graveside scene, a careening truck, or a childlike mother. But in her words, this is the truth she has chosen to own: "Trust God to turn the awfulness of the awful into ultimate wonder." Glorying in, rejoicing in God himself and his loving "personality" has become so absorbing that he carries, leads, energizes, and motivates her.

With the Spirit's help, Danette has discovered joy that grows out of the obedience of trusting. She has now completed a graduate degree in counseling so that she can help the hurting as she has been helped. She says that she doesn't expect life to be easy. She knows that restoration comes. She knows that peace can be resident even when life is unfair. I can imagine her authentically assisting others to discover that trust, and perhaps an early joy.

Dysfunctional families, disease, death, and all sorts of pain are the results of sin. We cannot take joy in them, but we can arrive at joy, as Danette has, because of God's ability to turn us around, to bring life out of death. He is ready, willing, and fully able to amaze us with invaluable results. We can be glad for the sweet, intimate knowledge of him that we know will come when we have been hurt at depth. Such hurt could drive us away, but if we choose, that very hurt moves us closer to him.

Unlike Danette, I was given a healthy home as a child. As a family, we sometimes went to the beach on the Atlantic coast, thirty minutes from home. It meant swimming (of sorts), and playing along the shore catching sand crabs and watching them scurry and burrow when I let them go. My skin stretched tightly by sunburn, I feasted on the best French fries anywhere and giggled in front of mirrors designed to distort one's image. I always found them along the boardwalk, and spent time convulsed with giggles at the six-hundred-pound image in the curving frames. "Weight loss" was easy. Just move to another mirror and become eight feet tall and fifty pounds; or watch your teeth grow longer than your legs.

To write "rejoice in suffering" across an actual mirror would be considered distorted graffiti. We do it to our "inner mirrors" when we emphasize the rejoice angle separate from a background of steady trust. We do it when rejoicing is forced too early in sorrow. We do it with good intentions, mistaken "kindness," and muddled orthodoxy. We do it in hospitals, after funerals, and on the way home from divorce courts.

We do it when we do not look carefully at the little word *in*. We are to rejoice *in* our sufferings. Does this mean we rejoice because of the sufferings themselves, that the sufferings are the cause or focus for rejoicing? Or does it mean that we can learn, as we move along in life, to rejoice in the middle of sufferings, as expressed by the poet:

> Before the winds that blow do cease,
> Teach me to dwell within Thy calm:
> Before the pain has passed in peace,
> Give me, my God, to sing a Psalm.[1]

Some folks earn an "F" in arithmetic when they add up Paul's ideas on this topic; they add up two plus two as anything but four, coming up with the following error:

1. Paul delights in difficulty and weakness.
2. Paul desires fellowship in Christ's own sufferings.
3. To Paul suffering is productive; it creates glory.
4. Sometimes "in" can mean "because of."
5. Paul means that we rejoice because of (in) sufferings themselves.

So two plus two equals five. Are we to rejoice in the affliction itself? Are we to rejoice in the rejection of divorce? Are we to be exuberant about suicide? Of course not. Are we to rejoice in the pain itself? Anyone who defends such a position has missed the point as Paul pushes toward the *result* of knowing God and honoring him in weakness in a way that we cannot when we are strong. In Scripture, there simply are not enough examples of "in" used to mean "because of" to push that idea. "Rejoicing in" means simply "in the middle of."

Mishandled, inaccurately thrown together, Paul's sentences force a poorly timed and glib "Praise the Lord." People tell Karen to "have faith," and make suggestions that sound as if she should thank God for multiple sclerosis, rheumatoid arthritis, blindness, and a miscarriage. I want to shout at them, "Karen *has* faith!" Occasionally people say too sweetly to her that "all things work for good," as if they have forgotten that all things work *together* for good. I want to scream: All things are not good.

If we look more closely we will find a way to scrub off the disturbing graffiti that well-meaning persons leave; not just painting over it, but totally erasing such grotesque distortions. Simply put: We rejoice in the middle of sufferings *knowing God and knowing the results.* Knowing him and actually knowing something of the results ahead of time enables us to develop a trusting joy in the middle of the hurt. We rejoice in sufferings because they produce perseverance, character, and the hope of glory.

One day I sat drinking coffee with Judith who told me the recent history of her son who, as an art student, had attended a major university. Each of his modern paintings invited one to "enter" through an open door, or to "bask" in shafts of light—thresholds and beams scoffed at by despairing fellow artists who had no place for hope on their palettes. At last, though, he couldn't carry on amid the criticism, and moved in other directions, which brought grief to his parents.

Judith talked for thirty minutes, answering my occasional questions and unconsciously communicating God's care "mid a thousand distresses."[2] God's faithfulness and goodness coupled with her trust were visible in her speech and in her attitude.

Then she said, "Now, I am trying to get at what 'rejoicing in suffering' means." I wanted to leap up right there and do a childlike ballerina twirl, laugh with her, and sing, and say, "But you know. You already know. You have shown me for thirty minutes. You have hope all over your personal canvas." The time and place were not right for such a performance, but I did it up quite well on the inside! And soon, we talked again.

Judith is as I was a few weeks ago. My Michigander friends, Mary and Stan, had sent flowers, just about ready to bloom with life in the dead of winter. The tulip bulbs were thrusting themselves out of the soil, tall green stems reaching toward the sunlit window. At first, I could see the shadow of my hand through the stems and I became fascinated with their transparency where they emerged from the bulbs. I was amazed at how fast they grew, and noticed that the blossoms, at first flat and thin, began to bulge a little. And I wished the tulips were daffodils. I love the way daffodils unknowingly trumpet their glory.

One morning we woke, and I staggered in typical morning stupor to the kitchen where I groped to plug in the ready-to-go percolator. I rounded the corner and there they were—daffodils in full bloom, laughing at me. Then, laughing with me. So carried away with the bulbs and their energetic outreach, I had not paid much attention to the buds. I don't know why I had assumed with such certainty that they were tulips because I wouldn't know a tulip from a daffodil bulb. Needless to say, I was delighted.

Judith knew she had planted bulbs of trust. She had searched Scripture for bulb boosters and had studied God's nature. But she hadn't recognized yet that the trust had burst out as rejoicing. Perhaps she was waiting for a whole brass band of rejoicing instead of a daffodil's soundless trumpet. A day came when Judith arrived at the certainty of relying on God, the joy of waiting on him for long-term results, momentarily invisible. As she spoke to me, she was characterized by sincere joy and peace. "I will boast all the more gladly about my weaknesses *so that* Christ's power may rest on me. . . . I delight in weaknesses, in insults, in hardships . . . for when I am weak, then I am strong" (2 Cor. 12:9–10).[3] Because I am earthen, God's power can shine through the cracks.

James also stresses results. "Consider it pure joy, my brothers, whenever you face trials . . . because you know that the testing of your faith develops perseverance. Perseverance must finish its work *so that* . . ." (1:2–4; emphasis mine).[4] James underlines "what the Lord finally brought about" in Job's life.

Peter agrees with Paul and James, saying, "In this you greatly rejoice, though now for a little while you may have had to suffer grief in all kinds of trials. These have come *so that* your faith—of greater worth than gold, which perishes even though refined by fire—may be proved genuine and *may result in* praise, glory and honor when Jesus Christ is revealed."[5]

It is as if, sitting here at the computer late on a Friday afternoon with a wintry sun sending light over my right shoulder, I were to type t-r-u-s-t, but God had programmed the computer to spell out j-o-y. I'm sure that if that were to happen, my mouth would drop open just as it did when the tulips "became" daffodils. Trust does eventually spell joy.

Steve Bruno could not have known how apt his description was when he wrote "Fog in the Desert."

When a rare fog visits my desert—usually on a wintry morning after a Pacific storm has passed—it can be surprisingly dense, a pervasive cloud reducing visibility to zero. It's then I lose all perspective and at times almost forget where I am. But most often it is irregular, patchy fog that lasts only a brief time, starting the day by reflecting the rosy sunshine.[6]

Just when we recognize that we are in a desert in the winter after a storm, wouldn't you know . . . fog socks us in. The desert, the winter, and the storm were plenty. When dense fog and reduced visibility are added, we lose our perspective and our orientation. If we choose, however, we can look for a hole in the fog. If we choose, we can *use* the fog and find reflected on the clouds a slight rosy hint, the radiance of our glorious God.

16

Rejoicing in God

"Africa held experiences I'd never trade. I remember our mountain-top hospital at Ingwavuma in the sunshine. Sometimes rainy, sometimes cool, I even recall lining our cars up, headlights on, to guide John, the pilot of our plane, as he landed in pervasive fog. The meaning came, not in exciting stories, but in getting to know God and in helping others know him. That's hard to convey in its actual significance, but knowing God meant, and means, everything."

June Salstrom, my good friend who also served in South Africa at our mission hospital, went on to tell of her African nickname, "Ntombi," which means "young girl." After many years in Africa, she wondered why she hadn't outgrown the name and asked some Zulu women to explain. They said it was rooted in the fact that she was the first single person to prove to them that a Christian could live a moral single life, and because of her example, they were willing to teach their young people to live by Scripture. Without her, they would have thought a pure life impossible; their knowledge of God would have been impaired!

Ntombi was amazed. The very issue that had sent her repeatedly to God for help and encouragement, asking him, "Why singleness?" was the key to their trusting God's power and the truth of Scripture! Her singleness was the motivating factor in their forming convictions that they would pass on to the next generation. She received a glimpse of what God was aiming at and, thus, never wished to avoid a path he had mapped out. Knowing God is everything to her, an encore for everyday.

> No one who has felt His rod would want to go that way again; but no one who has come with Job to "what the Lord is aiming at" . . . would ever wish not to have trodden His path.[1]

We have now come to *a* crucial point, if not *the* crucial point of this discussion: *Knowing God is everything.* We must know him well enough to know that he delights in kindness, that he enjoys beauty. We must know him well enough to begin to predict what he wants said and done. We must know him well enough to shudder at what makes him shudder, to weep at what makes him weep, to be moved at what moves him, to be pleased at behavior and results that please him. I must know him well enough to rejoice in his pleasure just as I delight, on a more mundane level, in fixing Jim's coffee exactly the way he likes it. Yes, God remains a sovereign God of startling surprises and serendipities, and I will never know his plans ahead of time, but I learn to glory in his well-loved nature just as I glory in the multifaceted personalities of my closest friends.[2]

When I saw the movie, *The Mission*, for the second time, it was with Ruth whom I know well and whose responses I can accurately forecast. I knew the film; I knew her. It was fun to realize that I knew so precisely what her reactions would be, and that in loving her, I had internalized some of them.

And so it is with God. Our knowledge of him becomes so intimate that we can begin to live with his pleasure in mind. And with him, as with earthly loved ones, a striking resemblance starts to develop. Sometimes I catch a facial expression of Jim's on my own face, or a tone in my voice that was initially his. We become like those we love, and our resemblance to God is urgently needed in order to display his nature to the world about us.

How can this sort of God-knowledge be encouraged? What is the most effective means of getting to know God? How can I arrive more quickly at this intimate, exquisite knowledge of him? I want to get on with it. What will make me stare at him, and scrutinize, and study him? What will help to rivet my gaze?

Suffering.

Suffering? Yes. The wealthy will eventually feel a need that dollars cannot touch. Billions of millions cannot buy top-of-the-line, state-of-the-art God contentment. The person who boasts inwardly and trusts his own wisdom, knowing what to say and do, and when to say and do it, will one day goof abominably. The people we know who are so well skilled interpersonally will run into someone whose personality paralyzes their outreach. Bodybuilders will someday notice a sag, a wrinkle, a pain, or a limitation. A friend will lose a friend. The happily married will lose a spouse. A basketball player will hurt his knee; a violinist, her hand. A treasured daughter will become a battered wife. We will suffer.

We will learn the folly of planning coronations for the self. Something will die inside, but knowing and understanding God brings on a "resurrection." Knowing God is everything, and I have known and will know him far, far better during and after pain. The continuity of my relationship with God through thick and thin becomes my cherished prize, a marvel in itself. Not that I ask for pain, but should it come, I use it as a shovel for digging hidden treasure. Habakkuk had the right idea:

> Though the fig tree does not bud
> > and there are no grapes on the vines,
> though the olive crop fails
> > and the fields produce no food,
> though there are no sheep in the pen
> > and no cattle in the stalls,
> yet I will rejoice in the LORD,
> > I will be joyful in God my Savior.
> > > Habakkuk 3:17–19

If knowing God indeed means everything, if that is my highest value, if that is my best-loved goal, then, in the long-term, the importance of the suffering itself will begin to shrink because suffering is a significant way in which to come to an intimate knowledge of God—a mental and a felt knowledge of his nature.

J. I. Packer tells of a friend who clashed with others over the gospel of grace and in so doing, limited his professional advancement. His friend's assessment was, "It doesn't matter, for I've known God, and they haven't."[3] Knowing God is everything.

Paul wrote, "I consider everything a loss compared to the surpassing greatness of knowing Christ Jesus my Lord, for whose sake I have lost all things. I consider them rubbish that I may gain Christ" (Phil. 3:8). Paul's inventory of grossly offensive rubbish consisted of numerous reasons he had once had for confidence in his own history and achievement. In the end, he considered everything to be loathsome garbage, with the one exception of knowing God. "What normal person spends his time nostalgically dreaming about manure?"[4] Knowing God is everything.

Wait a minute. Hold it. Hear me. Don't tell a weeping person (whether he is weeping outwardly or inwardly) that the aching loss "doesn't matter." It takes a great deal of living and perhaps some distance from the grief for a hurting person to be able to say such a thing. It takes the perspective that time and long reflection can bring. It requires healing that only the Spirit can offer; healing that is not, by the way, instantaneous. It requires long walks with God. It may require sobbing in his arms.

How I prayed that Arlene, Rev. Mac's widow, would be given space and time to grieve, that she would be allowed and encouraged to talk it out, that she would be given freedom to process emotion. We used to sing "It Is Well with My Soul" in that church. I hope that she still sings it now: "When sorrows like sea billows roll . . . it is well, it is well, with my soul."[5] I hope that she has given herself permission to cry real tears from a broken heart at the very time her soul is well. I hope that she and others who remember his death will be able to still ask questions knowing that their souls are "well," are at rest, because of God's unswerving care.

We do need time to process emotion and pain. Whisper the word, *rejoicing*, very softly when pain is actually in the room. The concept of rejoicing must be cut as it were from flannel-like cloth, soft enough to rest easily around its owner's form, and lined with trust. If you have earned a grieving person's trust, be ever so gentle, tender, careful, and sensitive with this idea of rejoicing so that it does not become a lethal weapon in your hands; so that it does not take the shape of an ugly mask, severe and harsh with artificial cheer.

In the presence of suffering, remember with quiet assurance that knowing God is everything, and that the one who suffers, whether you or someone else, will *eventually* reach that conclusion. This takes time—weeks, months, or even years. Whatever is required for a breadth and depth of the knowledge of God will finally be acceptable. It will be more than okay; it will gain your approval. His yoke will become easy, and one day his commands will become more like a weightless part of you than an external burden (Matt. 11:30; 1 John 5:3).

The central focus is this: Suffering is nothing compared with the surpassing greatness of knowing God. Count suffering as nothing, knowing God as everything. I am profoundly grateful that God brought me to this convinced position about three years before my marriage. I was able to say that singleness with its distress of loneliness, frustration, and apparent rejection was worth it for what I had learned of God by walking alone with him into my forties. This was a conclusion I *eventually* reached, and a conclusion eventually reached and maintained by Ntombi as she moves into her mid-sixties.

Suffering becomes rubbish or nothingness when it is set in contrast to the wonder of knowing God. And yet, we are to rejoice in it for its inestimable value in moving us to him. We can arrive like Paul in an "advanced state of holy indifference to pain,"[6] where knowing and exalting Christ is *all that matters*.

We have been looking at the wonder of knowing God from a human point of view. Philip Yancey turned this around in his study of our disappointment with God, trying to imagine how it feels for God to want a relationship with us. In fact, shortly after reading his book, I dreamed that while the paper jacket carried the title, *Disappointment with God*, I removed the jacket on our copy and saw that the actual title was, *Even in Our Pain, God Wants to Relate to Us*. Of course, no such thing happened, but it is one of Yancey's points.[7]

In and out of pain, this relationship goes on. You have seen pictures of the "before" and "after" in weight loss advertisements. If the "before," "during," and "after" of our interaction with God through our pain could be captured in a snapshot, we would see the weight coming off.

Believe me when I say that our relationship with God deepens. *I know God.* To me, that means everything, and without that fact, without that wonder, all else would mean nothing. With that wonder, how can we ever praise him enough!

17

R. S. V. P., The Majestic Glory

Glory to God! Amen and Amen! Glory to God who will lift our suffering forever. By now I hope you have joined me in a choir, a choral group that rejoices in God, that celebrates who he is and what he does.

Romans is not a funeral march or a dirge, but a celebration. Rejoicing reverberates three times in the first half of Romans 5. Remember that earlier, we decided Romans is like a brilliant concerto for organ and trumpet. The book may begin in a minor key, telling us the awful heinousness of sin, but it changes to a bright D-major key, and that is about as bright and joyful a key as a musician can find. Instead of wailing questions, even justifiable ones, into the darkness, we may sing with Annie Dillard:

My left foot says "Glory," and my right foot says "Amen," in and out of Shadow Creek . . . exultant, in a daze, dancing, to the twin silver trumpets of praise.[1]

Romans 5 is a *celebration*. Although Paul mentions suffering in Romans 5, he goes on to say that without Christ, we are powerless, ungodly, and sinful enemies of God. He writes of God's wrath and of Christ's blood and death. But there is more: Paul writes that God provides justification, reconciliation, faith, peace, access, grace, rejoicing, hope, patience, perseverance, and character. God cancels our disappointments and fills us with love expressed in the generosity of his poured-out Spirit." Praise God whose plan for salvation leads to glory. Limitless, amplified praise for God and his antecedent saving purpose!

From before creation, ahead of every other goal, God's top priority for us has been glory, our reflection of his glory, our participation in his glory in fellowship with him. He also calls believers who have fallen short to again *enjoy* his glory, to sing his glory, to dance to it, to revel in it. Those whom he calls, he justifies and *glorifies* (Rom. 3:23; 8:30).

God calls us. He invites us. Those of us who have come to Christ for salvation have replied to God's invitation and are already on our way into majestic glory. Praise for such a generous God. In Romans, Paul celebrates, throws a pre-heaven party, and invites us to come. By letting us in on the truth of Romans, he celebrates new birth and resurrection life.

Recently I had a birthday when my friends said that they are glad I was born; it was a day for me to thank God and my parents for the gift of life. It was also good for business at the local "blossom shop" because I received a corsage of red roses and white carnations from Jim, and a basket of perky flowers—purple irises, pink carnations, and daisies from Ruth. Both arrived wrapped in cardboard and paper that were rather uninteresting; I must confess that I didn't study the wrapping sufficiently to be able to tell you much about it. I tore into the paper, dropped it on the floor, and looked at the flowers. I wanted to get at the glory.

I also wanted to get at the names on the cards inside. God works in much the same way: He sends glory concealed in the disposable wrapping of suffering, and the card says, "Limitless love, from God." For now, for a little while yet, God's wrapping is a necessity. Sometimes he lets us see through the plain wrappings for a glimpse of his glory, but finally, one day, the first things will have been completely dispensed with, and there will be "no more death or mourning or crying or pain." He will wipe every tear from our eyes, and we will see his glory (Rev. 21:4).

Glory in the Old Testament sometimes refers to the presence or aura of a person, but most often it relates to the image or presence of God. Closely associated is the idea of light, luminous radiance, or splendor, and the effect of his presence and power. Glory is "something which radiates from the one who has it, leaving an impression behind." Used to describe God, *glory* refers to the "luminous manifestation of his person, his glorious revelation of himself," with stress laid on the created impression.[2] When Moses was on Mt. Sinai, "to the Israelites the glory of the LORD looked like a consuming fire on top of the mountain" (Exod. 24:17).

The New Testament meaning for glory remains close to the Old Testament meaning: Glory has its source in God, in his likeness, in his form or image, and glory is described in terms of radiance. It has to do with the power and activity of God, particularly his saving power. We "give God glory." We "glorify" him by recognizing who he is and admitting it through appropriate, accurate, and specific praise of his qualities.

Glory is a word to be reserved for the extraordinary. Don't dare speak to me of "glorious hamburgers," as a restaurant advertised not long ago. And use *glamour* for Hollywood, or for the jet-set, not the word *glory*. Save *glory* and glorious for the highest and best that connects to God. We have few untarnished words left to us; let *glory* remain shining, silvery, and clear.

John writes of Jesus' having glory in his telling us that Jesus is God. Bright light was a part of Paul's encounter with God on the Damascus Road, and Paul himself writes about Moses' radiance after he had been with God. Luke, in quoting Isaiah, includes God's saving activity as part of his glory.[3]

Can you think of any other word that encompasses all this? God's perfections, the "august contents . . . of God's entire nature . . . the aggregate of all his attributes" in their fullness![4] God not only *has* glory, but *is* glory; glory that awakens joy. By his very nature, he gives joy in overflowing communication, making himself conspicuous everywhere in nature so that all can see. God made himself conspicuous in Jesus Christ who is called "the Lord of glory."[5]

Such magnificent light and power could frighten us and send us scurrying away from him, but he works to draw us to him even in suffering; drawing us to the beauty and joy of glory, melting the distance into closeness. Paul tells us that our suffering is not worth comparing with the glory that will be revealed *in* us. God called us that we might "share in the glory of our Lord Jesus Christ" (Rom. 8:18; 2 Thess. 2:14). Those who believe God will actually participate in his glory.

"We who . . . reflect the Lord's glory, are being transformed into his likeness with ever increasing glory, which comes from the Lord, who is the Spirit." Ah . . . so that explains it! That is why I have already seen radiance on the faces of believers who are motherless or childless. They *are being* transformed. Though "outwardly we are wasting away, yet inwardly we are being renewed . . . for our light and momentary troubles are achieving for us an eternal glory that far outweighs them all." That's why I have already seen radiance in the lives of some who have lost spouses, or friends, or jobs, or health.[6]

Part of this radiance is the result of having one's "living channels" turned on by the Holy Spirit. Most of us enter adult life with at least one channel—choosing, thinking, feeling, or doing—jammed or weakened.[7] A person may be decisive in making choices or may be analytical and clear in thinking, but may not allow him- or herself to feel emotions. I talked to a young man like that recently. With a computer-like brain, he can remember, analyze, organize, and deliver vast stores of information. He claims to have some emotions, but the only sign I have seen of any was in the redness of his cheeks when I wondered aloud if he had been taught to squelch feelings.

Another person, aware and exercised emotionally, may be hesitant and indecisive when it is time to make plans or goals. Still another person may find it easy to change outward behavior (doing), but is slow to explore and investigate ideas, or to list options. Suffering enlivens and alerts all the channels.

The one who cannot identify with or experience feelings often begins to sense emotions in times of illness or loss. The individual who gave little time to serious thought and reflection begins to ask questions. Why this pain? The person who prefers to delay decisions learns how to make them when in distress. Whatever our weak channels are, they are strengthened by suffering. Whatever our dormant channels are, they are awakened, and with all these elements of lifestyle in working order, we are "quickened," or made alive. Abundance of life for the believer and the old-fashioned term, *quickening*, mean much, but in part they mean a healthiness, a readiness to be fully human, fully functional, fully alive.

For those whose center is God, loss and pain guarantee that they are fully alive. Eugene Peterson writes that our focus on God in prayer forces us to deal with reality and to live at a level of honesty unheard of by those who do not pray. He asks us if we are truly prepared to think that well and feel that deeply. "The Psalms take us to the painful heart of rejections and alienations and guilts that we could live on the surface of much more happily."[8]

Oddly enough, struggle and grief lead to a deepening of life and liveliness, guaranteeing for the committed believer glory, which seems to be pain's opposite. Rather than preventing glory, suffering ensures the appreciation and absorption of it. Victorious Christians do not need to hide tears in an unsuccessful attempt at forced radiance. They develop an inward trust that eventually leads to the real thing, glory now and in eternity.

There is glory now, and there will be glory then; glory already and glory not yet. There is glory that we attempt to imagine and comprehend, but it is glory that our eyes haven't seen and that no human mind has conceived (1 Cor. 2:9). There is glory "that is equally at home 'above the heavens' . . . and at the side of one forlorn person."[9] There is glory that is associated with the resurrection and life, but glory also relates to suffering and death. "The ministry that brought death . . . came with glory" (2 Cor. 3:7), and Jesus was "crowned with glory and honor because he suffered death" (Heb. 2:9).

The only time glory can be shown against a striking backdrop is now, in my suffering on earth. Far from shrinking when we contemplate suffering, in the here and now we are bound for Christ's sake "to gaze upon it . . . to see in it the turning point from death to life . . . to overlook suffering is to overlook Christ."[10]

What sincere believer would want to overlook Christ? No Christian can evade the turning point from death to life. Everything, even our doubts, desperation, private agonies, and anger turn a corner at last from death to praise.

> All prayer pursued far enough becomes praise . . . not a "word of praise" slapped onto whatever mess we are in at the moment . . . our prayers are going to end in praise . . . it is going to take a while. Don't rush it.[11]

Eugene Peterson writes this of the conclusion of the Psalms where hardy hallelujahs bounce off one another. But 149 other Psalms come first, Psalms that are parallel to the contemporary Christian's experience: praying, laughing, crying, doubting, believing, struggling, dancing, struggling again, and at the end "on our feet, applauding, 'Encore! Encore!'"[12]

One sentence that does not fit in the repertoire of spiritual struggle is: "I haven't got time for the pain." The person who habitually dodges difficulty and refuses to face his grief is not taking time to understand this "must" of life. Those who insist on ignoring the reality of loss, or abandonment, or struggle are in danger of overlooking Christ.

Alan Paton was a powerful prophet for twentieth-century South Africa; he spoke and wrote movingly with the aim of awakening other white people to the need for racial justice. Paton did not refuse struggle in the verbal battles he waged until his death in 1988. In the memoir he wrote for his wife, Dorrie, who had stood with him in all his efforts, Paton says, as if speaking to Dorrie,

> Where did your courage come from? It was . . . that strange Christianity of yours that took seriously the story of the Cross, that understood with perfect clarity that one might have to suffer for doing what one thought was right, that rejected absolutely that kind of crossless geniality that calls itself Christianity.[13]

Alan Paton's Christianity took time for the pain. He took a lifetime for pain, the pain of a Christ-follower, acquainted with grief. Jesus Christ took time for the pain, and Jesus Christ, the Man of Sorrows, is the King of Glory.

Paul wanted to "know Christ and the power of his resurrection and the fellowship of sharing in his sufferings, becoming like him in his death" (Phil. 3:10). What true believer would not want to be identified with Christ and to become like him? Christ was crowned with glory and honor because he was obedient. And our love for Jesus Christ means obedience. Obedience means sacrifice. Sacrifice means death to self. That death means life, resurrection life. Life becomes *the apparent thing* to onlookers because as the years go by, and we walk on and on with God, ever-increasing glory has a way of arousing curiosity and getting attention!

You and I have our limited, earthly ideas of glory but must work at understanding the glory that is described in the Bible. I dreamed once about "glory," but it was definitely my definition, not God's. Having read this far, you know that my values include deep relationships, and perhaps you've figured out that I like organ music. What you do not yet know is that I also enjoy eating out. One night a few years ago, I dreamed that these joys came together. Betty and Verleen, two of my organist friends, were with me in a restaurant, and they took turns playing a pipe organ for me while I ate. Oh, that would be glory for me! After a few numbers, I turned to them and asked if we could build three booths and live there, so that this wouldn't have to end!

Obviously, I had put Peter's idea at the transfiguration into my dream along with a human notion of what would constitute glory. Peter had quite a glimpse of glory, accurate where mine was not. He and James and John had gone with Jesus to pray, and as Jesus was praying, his face changed in appearance, "and his clothes became as bright as a flash of lightning." Peter wanted to build three shelters and stay right there, and was so impressed that he wrote about it later:

> We were eyewitnesses of his majesty. For he received honor and glory from God the Father when the voice came to him from the Majestic Glory, "This is my Son, whom I love; with him I am well pleased."
> 2 Peter 1:16–18 (in reference to Luke 9:29)

God's voice came from the Majestic Glory. Finally, one day, you and I as believers will be participants within that glory . . . if we are among those who said, "Yes" to God's R.S.V.P.

John, who shared the transfiguration experience, was privileged later to see a vision of heaven. He saw "a Lamb, looking as if it had been slain, standing in the center of the throne." He heard the voices of innumerable angels, singing,

"Worthy is the Lamb, who was slain,
to receive power and wealth and wisdom and strength and honor and glory and praise!"
And then he heard every creature in heaven and on earth and under the earth and on the sea, and all that is in them, singing:
"To him who sits on the throne and to the Lamb
be praise and honor and glory and power, for ever and ever!"
                                                            Revelation 5:13

What can we say to this glimpse of glory? We can only say, "Amen," and fall down before the throne to worship the Father and Jesus Christ, who with his blood purchased men for God from every tribe and language and people and nation. We follow and praise and worship God's *slain* Lamb, the King of *Glory*.

18

Smitten by Glory

All, who have believed God throughout all time, sing: "Glory to God. Amen and Amen." We sing and march to the rhythm of truth, to a majestic, ceremonial march. "Man's chief end is to glorify God, and to enjoy Him for ever."[1] The highest goal is not that we be made holy and glorious, as transformed believers, but rather that God's name be honored. We step back from the center of the picture, so that God may have his place, so that God receives glory.[2]

Glory is a word that I do not use lightly, but the crown jewels of England qualify as "glorious." They wait in sparkling splendor to be admired at the Tower of London. As I stood in line several years ago to see them, there was time to do a fair amount of people watching and even time to study the vault in which the jewels are kept. The walls of that vault are at least a foot thick, and one soon notices the steel reinforcements as well as the massive door with its impressive locks. Why all this for a few jewels?

The jewels answered my question when I finally rounded the corner into the room. There were diamonds, sapphires, emeralds, gold, scepters, crowns, gem-laden swords—all gleaming emblems of royalty and majesty. The Star of Africa on the Scepter with the Cross is reputedly the largest cut diamond in the world, with 530 carats and 74 facets.[3] The Orb of England, a gold sphere trimmed with pearls, diamonds, emeralds, rubies, and an amethyst, radiantly symbolizes the dominion of Christianity.[4] St. Edward's Crown, weighing seven pounds, was so heavy that Queen Victoria ordered the lighter Imperial State Crown with its mere three thousand jewels.[5] These were the trimmings that garnish a ceremonial occasion; the symbols of a sovereign; the adornment that makes a regal Queen Elizabeth more regal.

We were instructed to walk in a circle, single file, around a central pillar that was itself covered with mirrors. The jewels were displayed in front of the mirrors and protected by special glass. Fascinated folks who held up the progress of the line were encouraged by uniformed guards to take another unwilling step. One saw not only the front of a particular gem, but many angles of others because the display case had eight sides. The backs of the jewels sparkled in the mirrors' reflections. The tour was well worth my twenty pence, the price in 1977.

Just as the entry fee has soared, that experience has grown in value for me, value inappropriate for monetary measurement. I see now that as I progress through life, its various circumstances allow me to view the nature of God from many perspectives. Countless situations are required even to begin to display the priceless infinity of sparkling "jewels," jewels of radiant splendor and ultimate value; glory himself. Knowing God is everything.

Once I stared at him even as I wept because of an injured friendship. Through red eyes, I saw him with arms outstretched to receive me, and I saw his Son outstretched on a cross, rejected. Slowly moving on, I saw other facets of his resplendent character. From the perspectives of a treasured bride or a warmly accepted friend, I have seen and felt what his love is like. Looking at God from a new vantage point did not mean forgetting the other facets I had seen, for they were viewed at still other angles.

Sharing another's grief at a loss through death, I know him as the God of all comfort. Rejoicing in a loved one's health report, I recognize an all-powerful God who can heal. Wincing when I think of a little girl's surgery, I gaze thankfully at a God who stays by her, walks along the hospital hallway, and enters the operating room to hold her small hands. And yet, present everywhere, he stays to comfort me as I hurt for her!

And now I find God big enough to heal my hurt and dissolve my anger. His energy and vitality encourage me when my vigor leaks away. I walk on the edge of his wisdom when decisions loom immediately ahead, and I draw on his patience when impatience tries to consume me. I sense his presence when friends are absent, and I sense his presence differently when they are nearby to comfort me. In pervasive fear, he is my courage. I do not know all the answers, but faith based on who he is helps me manage the uncertainty. Knowing God is everything.

That day in England, a spokesman for the Crown said, "Move ahead, please." I obeyed.

Now as I go on obeying God's voice, I am amazed at further discoveries of other aspects of his jeweled grandeur. I am learning to participate in glory. I am charmed by God's beauty. I am awestruck. I am captivated. I am stunned.

Though I still hurt, I trust God, and he enables me to move from the trusting aspect of rejoicing into the fuller reality of joy. Yes, I rejoice in him and in the solid hope of his glory.

Epilogue

Alan Paton writes that there are "lights along a dark and sorrowful road; and by the grace of God, it is the lights that one remembers."[1] Paton wrote this during his first year of grief after his wife's death.

I agree with Paton that one remembers the lights along the dark road. The evidence is there in Bibles and hymnals that I have saved from my past. As new versions have become available, or my studies have changed my tastes, I have kept old Bibles and hymnals as records, because their margins help me remember specific interventions of God's grace. I have just chosen a dusty Bible from the bookcase, the Bible that I used in the early years in South Africa, and it fell open at the Psalms. I see that "June 3, 1971" is scribbled next to Psalm 93.

The rivers have risen, O LORD; the streams have swirled up with their roar; the floods are surging high. Above the sound of expansive waters, of mighty ocean breakers, the LORD on high stands supreme.

Psalm 93:3–4 (Berkeley)

171

On June 3, 1971, I apparently needed Psalm 93, but now more than twenty years later, I wonder why. I have no idea what that day's dilemma was, but I know that for many years, Psalm 93 has been a light for me.

When I turn the pages of my favorite hymnal with its tattered binding, I find "F.L., October 14, 1978," written next to *God Moves in a Mysterious Way*.[2] The notation tells me that Fern Larson and I sang it together on that date. The stimulus to sing "The clouds ye so much dread are big with mercy and will break with blessing on your head" may have been that I was adjusting to life in the United States again, though Ingwavuma, Natal, South Africa, still felt like home. Fern was returning to South Africa. As I developed my new identity as a student, no longer being a missionary, the clouds did break in mercy. More than fifteen years later, I recall almost nothing of the growing pains of adjustment, but I can still tally the blessings.

Yes, blessings accumulate and light diffuses over our paths as we walk on with God, but there is a danger when we begin to remember only the light and forget the dark that caused us to call on God in the first place. The danger is that we will try to pull people who are currently hurting into our accumulated light too quickly. This would concern me today because this is my last day to polish the final draft of this book, and I fear that my light, gathered for years, could blind people who are hurting. But this morning I am a person in pain.

All I can do is trust and cry. I feel no joy, and I am disoriented because we received bad news last week. We learned that seven months from now Jim, along with several others, will no longer have his position at the seminary, due to severe budget cuts.

Something within us died. Today, we feel robbed of our future.

Stripped from us in these losses is the sense of security, worth, and belonging that related to our work. Far less important losses are the house that is our home and our comfortable familiarity with this city. We will leave our new lilac bush and saplings, trees more newly planted than we are. We wanted to nurture them and watch them mature, even as we wanted to nurture and watch our students mature.

Two mornings after we were told the news, I woke with an unexpected verse printed on the computer screen of my brain:

> The Lord Jesus, on the night he was betrayed, took bread, and when he had given thanks, he broke it and said, "This is my body, which is [broken] for you."
>
> 1 Corinthians 11:23–24

The kingdom was not on my mind when God printed First Corinthians 11:23–24 on my mental screen that morning. The most significant thought for me at that time was the fact that Jesus turned to God on the same night he was betrayed. Because of this I have been reminded of something I had written long ago: In the painful pauses of our lives, our on-going conversation with God is the important factor.

Thinking of First Corinthians 11, I converse with God, saying, "This is my heart, broken for you." I want to wait on God in this pause when time seems to have stopped. I want God to be more important to me than job security. True security does not flow from our work.

These are days when I ask myself questions. Am I more resilient now than eleven years ago when I began to study the passages in Romans? I answer with vigor, "Yes, undoubtedly." Do I still believe all that I have written, prior to our loss, in this book? Yes, I believe it all, and am grateful for these truths, more thankful than I have ever been.

God is still teaching me to trust, and I know that trust will breed joy. I trust that he will one day take this shock and work it together, with all the facets of our lives, for good, in the strongest and best sense of the word "good." I am living in a sacred situation of pain, choosing to work through the process involved in grieving, and expecting this process to require time and energy. I trust God to help me embrace this change as "a severe mercy," severe for now, merciful in the long run.[3] It is as if I hear faintly the deep bong of an enormous church bell that rings out hope; the bell rings at the edge of my perceptions, barely within my range of hearing, but I sense the vibrations. And even with this hope, even when suffering promises excellent results because of God's chemistry, my suffering hurts.

The thoughts and suffering of these weeks are like those I experienced years ago when that family moved away, losing me without grief, or so it seemed. The difference now is my knowledge of handling the pain of loss, my ability to process grief, especially by taking one major step: Now I know how to turn more quickly to God in his sensitivity and beauty. And I know how effective it can be to foster gratitude by searching out his beauty on the earth.

Since last week I have watched the sparrows at our bird-feeder for several minutes at a time. I am told in Scripture to "Look at the birds, free and unfettered, not tied down to a job description, careless in the care of God" (Matt. 6:26). I want to be steeped in the "God-reality, God-initiative, (and) God-provisions" of Matthew 6:33, so I watch the sparrows.[4] God says to me that surely if he knows how to feed and care for these plain little birds, he knows how to feed and care for a human being like me, made in his image.

After the bad news came, the Lord's Prayer of Matthew 6 kept coming to mind. This prayer, known from childhood, has deepened in significance in these days because my thoughts are scattered and wandering, and this prayer helps me to focus. "Our Father in heaven, hallowed be your name." Yes, no matter what happens, you are my father, and you deserve glory. Jesus' words express for me my deep desire: "Your kingdom come, your will be done." And when I think about the small number of positions available in a time of retrenchment for many schools, I ask that he give us our daily bread. When I resist forgiving people involved in letting us go, I must say, "Forgive us our trespasses, as we forgive those who trespass against us." I trust God to remind me again how to forgive. Then I come to "Lead us not into temptation," and pray against the temptation to take just any positions in order to have someplace to go. I pray against the temptation to take positions with a prestigious school if the right positions are in an obscure corner. And I arrive at "Deliver us from evil," asking that we not damage the reputations of others by the use of our tongues in gossip and that we not allow a root of bitterness to take hold (Heb. 12:15).

By the time I have prayed the Lord's Prayer a few times in my mind with this sort of meaning in its lines, I am quiet. And by the time I have prayed it a few more times, I center on "Father . . . your kingdom come, your will be done," for that is at the core of every request. And a few moments later, I am satisfied with the one word "Father," which conveys to me that God is my reality, that God will take initiative, and that God is my provider.

Suffering is a "must" in the Christian's life, but as we center our focus on God, we find that trust is a necessity. To trust God, to entrust myself to him, means to turn myself fully toward him and place my "center of gravity" in him.[5] This trust is only the first step toward rejoicing and may involve waiting before joy returns in full.

Notes

Chapter One: *Test Cases for Truth*
1. Annie Dillard, *Pilgrim at Tinker Creek* (New York: Harper's Magazine Press), 1974, 8. Annie Dillard interprets nature as Virginia Stem Owens does in *Wind River Winter* (Grand Rapids: Zondervan Publishing House, 1987). Each author serves up creation in terms of suffering, beauty, hope, joy, and glory.
2. J. Christiaan Beker, "Suffering and Triumph in Paul's Letter to the Romans," *Horizons in Biblical Theology* 7, 2, (December 1985): 106.
3. Scots Metrical version of the Bible, Psalm 147:3.
4. The Bible is inspired, "God-breathed, and is useful for teaching, rebuking, correcting, and training in righteousness" (2 Tim. 3:16), and is infallible, without error in the original manuscripts. This ensures our acceptance of what Paul has written, but when you and I have hurt, we call on Paul as a fellow sufferer and learn to appreciate his specific afflictions.

Chapter Two: *Unexpected Exit, Unbroken Hope*
1. This book is not written to answer all questions about suicide, but it is clear that Scripture tells us murder is wrong

because human beings are made in God's image. This can be extended to include the wrongness of murdering oneself (Gen. 9:6; Exod. 20:13, 21:12; Job 1:21; 1 Cor. 6:19–20). See J. T. Clemens, "Suicide," in *The International Standard Bible Encyclopedia* (Grand Rapids: Eerdmans, 1956), 4:652–53.

Scripture says that "the unpardonable sin" is blasphemy against the Holy Spirit, not suicide as many have thought (Matt. 12:31). Rev. Mac could have died, begging forgiveness and praying for his family, even as he killed himself. If mental confusion prevented that, he had still confessed Christ as Savior, admitted his own personal sinfulness and need of salvation, and he knew whom he believed. He was convinced that God was able to guard what he had entrusted to Christ on earth and in heaven through all time and eternity. Nothing could separate Rev. Mac from the love of Christ (2 Tim. 1:12; Romans 8:38–39).

2. Barbara Faught, "When Jesus Lifts the Fog," *Christian Week* 6, 1 (April 14, 1992): 7.

3. See David Neff, "The Suicide Machine, *Christianity Today* 34, 11 (August 20, 1990): 14.

Chapter Three: *My Story*

1. Amy Carmichael, *Toward Jerusalem* (Fort Washington, Pa.: Christian Literature Crusade, 1936), 6.

2. Karl Barth, *The Epistle to the Romans*, trans. Edwyn C. Hoskyns (London: Oxford University Press, 1933), 156. For more along these lines, read J. I. Packer, "What Do You Mean When You Say God?" *Christianity Today* 30, 13 (September 19, 1986): 27–31.

3. Karl Barth, quoted by G. F. Hawthorne, in *Philippians*, Word Bible Commentary (Waco: Word, 1983), 183–84; italics mine.

4. Henri J. M. Nouwen, *Out of Solitude* (Notre Dame: Ave Maria, 1974), 57.

5. See Eugene H. Peterson, *Answering God* (San Francisco: Harper and Row, 1989), 63.

My move from verse 6 to 7 of Psalm 4 came after years of reading Thompson's *The Hound of Heaven*; the pursuit of a loved one by God. This is my favorite section:

> All which I took from thee I did but take,
> > Not for thy harms,
> But just that thou might'st seek it in my arms.
> > All which thy child's mistake
> Fancies as lost, I have stored for thee at home:
> > Rise, clasp my hand, and come!
> > Halts by me that footfall:
> > Is my gloom, after all,
> Shade of his hand, outstretched caressingly?
> > Ah, fondest, blindest, weakest,
> > I am he whom thou seekest!
> Thou dravest love from thee, who dravest me.

"Dravest" in the previous verse is the past tense of drive, (drove away).

6. See Ephesians 1:18–21 on the power of the resurrection. It is not that our sharing his sufferings is like Christ's in his death for the sins of the world. We are not redeemed by our suffering, but we do suffer for his sake, and we suffer as we die to sin in our lives. There is inward, spiritual grief as we live in a world hostile to our Lord, and there will be outward struggle.

Philippians 3:10 refers to Christ's sufferings and our entering into fellowship with him, while Romans 5 speaks more broadly of all kinds of suffering. According to either passage, the suffering of the believer can lead to a more intimate knowledge of God. Additional information on the words used in the New Testament for *suffering* will be given later.

7. The idea of "hope taking over" will be expressed in many ways here. By that, I do *not* mean that hope and relief from the burdens we carry (help given by God) will result in self-centered luxuriating. "The relief of private burdens is to set the person free to assume more important and universal ones," such as injustice, hunger, others' ills and anxieties. Daniel

Day Williams, *The Minister and the Care of Souls* (New York: Harper & Row, 1961), 25–26. See also Kenneth Leech, *Soul Friend*, (San Francisco: Harper, 1977), 102–3.

Chapter Four: *Paul's Life at Thorn's Point*

1. I am including only the sufferings recorded by Paul, which preceded his writing of Romans, since we are looking primarily at Romans chapters 5 and 8.

2. That a strong man like Paul could become afraid may seem surprising, but he admits to fear in 1 Corinthians 2:3. The Greek of the prohibition in Acts 27:24, where the angel tells him not to fear, points to the fact that he was already afraid. Suffering may not be as bad as our fear of it, or to some people fear may be a form of suffering.

3. 2 Corinthians 12:1–2; 1:8–9; Galatians 2:11–21; 1 Thessalonians 2:17–3:5; 1:7–12.

4. Philippians 3:7–11. R. Alan Cole discusses Paul's secret and the parallels in Paul's life to the sufferings of Christ, in "The Life and Ministry of Paul," in *The Expositor's Bible Commentary*, ed. F. E. Gaebelein (Grand Rapids: Zondervan, 1979), 1:557–73. Of course, our sufferings and Paul's are not redemptive as Christ's were, and we are not forwarding redemptive history in the same way that Paul did.

5. 2 Corinthians 8:2; Ephesians 3:13; Colossians 1:24; 1 Thessalonians 1:6; italics mine.

Chapter Five: *Facing the Facts*

1. Herman Ridderbos, *Paul, An Outline of His Theology* (Grand Rapids: Eerdmans, 1975), 251.

2. Paul had other reasons for bringing Abraham into Romans 4, but he does serve as an excellent illustration for our discussion, and this account immediately precedes Romans 5.

3. C. S. Lewis, *Weight of Glory* (Grand Rapids: Eerdmans, 1965), 2. Another author named Lewis explains the route back to glory: "The 'how' is a derivative of the 'why.' God's 'end' is the securing of 'sons.' . . . [This] purpose

reached back to motivate not only the initial creative step
... but also all the other countless steps ... decisions, crises,
frustrations, pressures, disciplines, limitations, risks, chas-
tisements ... to appear within the vast process that would
connect the end with the beginning. Futility is the ground
not of despair but of hope." Edwin Lewis, "A Christian
Theodicy: An Exposition of Romans 8:18–39," *Interpretation* 11, 4 (1957): 405.

Chapter Six: *Forgiven and Accepted*

1. Philip Yancey, *Disappointment with God* (Grand
Rapids: Zondervan, 1991), 183. Yancey tells of Paul Brand's
reply to the question, "Where is God when it hurts?" Brand
answered, "He is in you, the one hurting, not in it, the thing
that hurts."

2. David Hill, *Greek Words and Hebrew Meanings: Studies in the Semantics of Soteriological Terms* (London: Cambridge University Press, 1967), 160.

3. Cranfield, *Commentary on the Epistle to the Romans,*
The International Critical Commentary (Edinburgh: Clark,
1975), 1:258, 267.

4. Barth, *Epistle to the Romans,* 149, 155.

Chapter Seven: *From Faith to Faith*

1. Rabbi Heschel, quoted by Philip Yancey, in *Disappointment with God* (Grand Rapids: Zondervan Publishing
House, 1988), p. 208. Yancey has studied Scripture and life
and has done extensive homework in both. *Disappointment
with God* is a foundation for *When Teardrops Dance,* and is
especially for the person who is asking "Is God silent? Unfair? Hidden?" Yancey's book, *Where Is God When It Hurts?*
(Grand Rapids: The Zondervan Corporation, 1977), is his
earlier balanced response to human pain.

2. Yancey, *Disappointment with God,* 206–7.

3. J. Christiaan Beker, *Paul, the Apostle: The Triumph of
God in Life and Thought* (Philadelphia: Fortress, 1980), 75.

Romans was written to Christian believers, so the discussion in this book relates primarily to Christians.

4. Ernst Kasemann, "'The Righteousness of God' in Paul," *New Testament Questions Today* (London: SCM Press, 1969), 169–70. In Philippians 3, where Paul makes his statement about wanting to know Christ and the power of his resurrection and the fellowship of his suffering, he is also discussing righteousness.

5. Romans 5:1–11; 8:17–30. William Sanday and Arthur C. Headlam, *A Critical and Exegetical Commentary on the Epistle to the Romans* (Edinburgh: Clark, 1902), 125.

6. J. I. Packer, *Knowing God* (London: Hodder and Stoughton, 1973), 275, 279.

7. Ibid., 279.

8. John B. Dykes, "Holy, Holy, Holy," in *Worship and Service Hymnal* (Chicago: Hope Publishing Company, 1967), 105.

Chapter Eight: *The Cross at the Center*

1. I am referring to the "divine must," (Greek *dei*), which is not given in a specific verse, but is seen throughout Scripture. In discussing the divine must of suffering, we must note Lamentations 3:33–39: "He does not willingly bring affliction or grief to the children of men." We bring it on ourselves! See also Lamentations 3:39, Hebrews 12, and Luke 24:26, as well as Reinier Schippers' article "Persecution," in *The New International Dictionary of New Testament Theology*, ed. Colin Brown (Grand Rapids: Zondervan, 1975), 2:808; Burkhard Gartner, "Suffer," in *The New International Dictionary of New Testament Theology*, 3:724; and Acts 9:16; 14:22; 1 Thessalonians 3:3; 1 Peter 2:21.

2. John R. W. Stott, "God on the Gallows," *Christianity Today* (January 16, 1987): 1, 28–30, 31.

3. Madeleine L'Engle, *The Other Side of the Sun* (New York: Farrar, Straus, and Giroux, 1971), 45.

We are so ready to fight the necessity of suffering. Writing of necessities such as food, clothing, shelter, and warmth, which require death—the loss of animals and trees—in creation around us, Virginia Stem Owens says we must learn to accept our necessities with humility. I believe we must learn to accept the necessity of suffering. We need to learn to accept suffering with humility, the humility of persons for whom the Son of God died (Owens, *Wind River Winter*, 41).

4. L'Engle, *The Other Side of the Sun*, 143, 146.

5. Owens, *Wind River Winter*, 16.

6. Packer, *Knowing God*, 217–18.

7. Michael Pountney, "The Certainty of Nails," *Christian Week*, 6, 1 (April 14, 1992): 5.

8. Verses from Romans are included without designation in this section to prevent breaking the flow of thought; see Romans 4:25; 5:1, 6, 8, 10.

9. Kenneth Leech, *Soul Friend* (San Francisco: Harper, 1977), 37.

Chapter Nine: *Suffering, a Sacred Situation*

1. Genesis 35:1–7; 42:21; Exodus 4:31; Deuteronomy 28:53; 1 Samuel 1:6; 2 Samuel 22:19; Nehemiah 9:27; Psalm 107:39; Exodus 3:9–10. Derek Kidner, *Psalms 1–72*, ed. D. J. Wiseman (Downer's Grove, Ill.: InterVarsity Press, 1973), 234.

2. Beth Spring, "How Kathryn Koob's Faith Sustained Her As Captive," *Christianity Today*, 25, 5 (March 13, 1981): 61–64. David M. Alpern et al, "444 Days in Captivity," *Newsweek*, 97, 6 (February 9, 1981): 28–39.

3. Matthew 13:21; 24:9; John 16:21; Acts 7:9–11; 11:19; 20:23; 2 Corinthians 7:5; 8:2, 13; James 1:27.

4. *Pathema* is Paul's choice for Romans 8:18, but *thlipsis* is the stronger word in that it is less vague. Second Corinthians 1:4–6 shows *thlipsis* and *pethema* as descriptive of our sufferings. Colossians 1:24 speaks of the sufferings of Christ (*thlipsis*) and of the believer (*pathema*). *Stenochoria* is linked with *thlipsis* in three New Testament appearances and seems the stronger of the two words, serving to heighten *thlipsis*; see 2 Corinthians 4:8 and 2 Corinthians 6:4. Murray Harris writes of Paul's troubles as oppressive experiences, his hardships as un-

relieved adverse circumstances, and his distresses as tight corners (*en thlipsesin, en anagkais, ev stenochoriais*). Murray Harris, "II Corinthians," *The Expositor's Bible Commentary*, 10:357.

5. I have borrowed "sacred situation" from Tilden Edwards, *Spiritual Friend, Reclaiming the Gift of Spiritual Direction* (New York: Paulist, 1980), 130.

Chapter Ten: *Frustration's Goal: Freedom at Last*

1. Bob and Martha Baptista, *Ric* (Chicago: Moody Press, 1981), 143.

2. O. Bauernfein, "Mataios," *Theological Dictionary of the New Testament*, ed. Gerhard Kittel (Grand Rapids: Eerdmans, 1964), 4:523.

3. Hans-Georg Link, "Weakness," in *The New International Dictionary of New Testament Theology*, 3:993–94.

Chapter Eleven: *The Pause That Progresses*

1. Psalm 84:5–7. Derek Kidner, *Psalms 73–150*, ed. D. J. Wiseman (Downers Grove, Ill.: InterVarsity Press, 1973), 305. 1 John 3:2; 2 Corinthians 3:18.

2. John Calvin comments on patience not being the natural result of tribulation in *Commentaries on the Epistle of Paul the Apostle to the Romans* (Grand Rapids: Eerdmans, 1947), 191.

The considerable interplay in the words faith, hope, waiting, and patience, can be uncovered by using a good concordance, alongside the Bible, or by studying *The New International Dictionary of New Testament Theology*, 4 vol., ed. Colin Brown (Grand Rapids: Zondervan Publishing House, 1975).

3. Thomas Oden, *Guilt-Free* (Nashville: Abingdon, 1980), 70–71.

4. Virginia Stem Owens, *Wind River Winter*, 16. Later Owens differentiates between saints who sacrifice all, early in life, and the rest of us who "go the long way round . . . through intention, desire, ambition, achievement—and the

shadow side of each. Through human closeness and its cloying. Through weariness and defeat," 87.

5. Oden, *Guilt-Free*, 70–75.

I am adding fear-free to Oden's guilt-free, because our specific guilts and fears reveal our personal values. Robert Morosco writes that fear stands on two legs, and the legs are almightiness (power) and impendency (presence). The object of fear has power of some sort and seems to be present or approaching us quickly. Breaking either of its legs, power or presence, leaves fear inoperative. As believers, we find the power and presence of God sufficient to disable our fears, or we discover in God the wisdom and courage to disable the fears ourselves. In this process, our knowledge of God and his nature is clarified, and we learn to trust in him as he truly is. Robert Morosco, "Theological Implications of Fear," in *Wholeness and Holiness*, ed. H. Newton Maloney, (Grand Rapids: Baker, 1983), 118–127.

Rev. Marty Voltz, in a message on "Freedom From Fear" at North Suburban Evangelical Free Church in Deerfield, Illinois, told us that God, in response to the people's fears in the book of Exodus, assured them of his presence, power, and ultimate glory.

Hannah Hurnard names her main character "Much Afraid" in *Hind's Feet in High Places*. At first, Much Afraid is given two companions named "Suffering" and "Sorrow;" then when God completes his work in Much Afraid, her name is changed to "Grace and Glory." *Hind's Feet in High Places*, (London: Olive Press, 1955).

6. Virginia Stem Owens, *Wind River Winter*, 25.

7. Amy Carmichael, *Edges of His Ways*, (Fort Washington, Pa.: Christian Literature Crusade), 100.

8. Virginia Stem Owens, *Wind River Winter*, 80.

9. Bradford Torrey, "Not So In Haste, My Heart," 1875.

10. Cranfield, *A Critical and Exegetical Commentary on the Epistle to the Romans*, 1:261.

11. Peter T. White, "Gold, the Eternal Treasure," *National Geographic Magazine* 145, 1 (January 1974): 16.

12. The NIV renders this "character," in Romans 5:3–4; KJV, "experience"; NASV, "proven character"; NEB, "proof that we've stood the test."

13. Gleason Archer writes that Job's error was in "drawing conclusions on the basis of mere appearances." He tells us that Job "challenged God in three areas: the worthwhileness of allowing a baby to live who would . . . become the victim of such affliction; . . . the kindness or fairness of God; . . . the justice of God." Gleason L. Archer, *The Book of Job: God's Answer to the Problem of Undeserved Suffering* (Grand Rapids: Baker, 1982), 110. It is important to note that Job disputed God's very nature (his wisdom, kindness, fairness, and justice); my emphasis here is that suffering teaches us of God's nature if we are willing students.

14. Gilbert A. Peterson, *The Christian Education of Adults* (Chicago: Moody Press, 1984), 49.

Chapter Twelve: *Hope, Certain and Solid*

1. Walther Zimmerli, *Man and His Hope in the Old Testament* (London: SCM Press, 1971), 9. Though trust is the primary element in biblical hope, there is a forward look in hope toward the events of the Last Days; Isaiah 25:9; 42:4; 51:5; Jeremiah 29:11; Micah 7:7; Habakkuk 2:3.

2. E.g., Hosea 2:15, "I . . . will make the Valley of Achor a door of hope." *Achor* means "trouble."

One must study *hope* carefully to "fine tune" it in each passage. It is illegitimate to take the meaning in different chapters of Scripture, add them up to reach one large definition, and then transfer the total back into each passage.

3. Colossians 1:27; Ephesians 2:12; 1 Timothy 1:1; 1 Thessalonians 1:3; Romans 5:9–11; 8:23; 1 Corinthians 15, particularly verse 19; Galatians 5:5; Philippians 3:21.

4. Zimmerli, *Man and His Hope in the Old Testament*, 4. Using a different mental image, C. F. D. Moule in *The Meaning of Hope* (Philadelphia: Fortress, 1963), 19, says we must

"cast ourselves trustfully into the deep which is God's character. To hug the shore is to cherish a disappointing hope; . . . to swim is to discover the bouyancy of hope," again—God's character.

5. Henry Wadsworth Longfellow, "The Wreck of the Hesperus," in *The Poetical Works of Longfellow*, Cambridge Edition, (Boston: Houghton Mifflin, 1975), 13–14.

6. Josef Scharbert, "Suffering," in *Sacrementum Verbi*, ed. Johannes Bauer (New York: Herder and Herder, 1970), 3:892. Katherine, a concert pianist in *A Severed Wasp*, by L'Engle, listens to an elderly bishop tell of his experiences in war where his task was to remove the bodies of fallen soldiers from the battlefield. He says, "Why didn't I wipe God out, once and for all? There's nothing abominable I didn't see and hear . . . When things go well, we don't cry out for God as we did then, in anguish, in rage. I was closer to God in my abysmal nakedness of soul than I was when I was consecrated bishop. We get complacent and self-satisfied. Alas. But when you're in the middle of hell you don't have choice." Madeleine L'Engle, *A Severed Wasp*, (New York: Farrar, Straus, and Giroux, 1982), 88–89.

Chapter Thirteen: *The Crux of the Matter*

1. Herman Ridderbos, *Paul, An Outline of His Theology* (Grand Rapids: Eerdmans, 1975), 251.

2. There is a difference in knowing Christ and knowing information. To know Christ means to be brought under his influence in a personal relationship with personal contact. "This is eternal life: that they may know you, the only true God, and Jesus Christ . . ." (John 17:3).

3. Ridderbos, *Paul, An Outline of His Theology*, 489.

4. See also Martin Luther, *Commentary on the Epistle to the Romans* (Grand Rapids: Zondervan, 1954), 158.

5. Our discussion here is limited to believers, because Romans 5 and 8 is limited in this way. Stott, on page thirty in "God on the Gallows," reminds us that God's sympathy is not only for Christians. He notes that Jesus said we would be minister-

ing to him in ministering to the hungry and thirsty, the stranger, the naked, the sick, and the prisoner; Matthew 25:31–46.

6. Baptista, *Ric*, 147.

7. Kidner, *Psalms 73–150*, 259–60, on Psalm 73.

8. Ibid., 305, Psalm 84:5–7. "Valley of Weeping" is the Revised Version's translation based on the Septuagint. NIV gives "Valley of Baca," in reference to trees or shrubs growing in arid places. NEV gives "the thirsty valley." Kidner says that making this valley a place of springs is "a classic statement of the faith that dares to dig blessings out of hardships."

9. The statistics on bitterness as the number one cause of burn-out come from research by Frank Minirth and Paul Meier. See their book, *How to Beat Burn-out* (Chicago: Moody Press, 1986), particularly the chapters, "Bitterness: A Hidden Root," and "The Rekindling of Hope."

10. Owens, *Wind River Winter*, 23.

11. John 8:31–32. C. S. Lewis, *Mere Christianity*, 172–73. "From the outset that the goal towards which He is beginning to guide you is absolute perfection, and no power in the whole universe, except you yourself, can prevent Him from taking you to that goal . . . We may be content to remain what we call ordinary people, but He is determined to carry out quite a different plan. To shrink back from that plan is not humility; it is laziness or cowardice. To submit to it is not conceit or megalomania; it is obedience."

12. Paul Welter gives hurting people time to process their emotions throughout *How to Help A Friend* (Wheaton: Tyndale House, 1978).

13. Derek Kidner, *Psalms 1–72*, ed. D. J. Wiseman (Downers Grove, Ill.: InterVarsity Press, 1973), 213.

14. Peterson, *Answering God*, 87.

15. Second Corinthians 4:7. Luci Shaw, *The Sighting* (Wheaton: Harold Shaw, 1981), 28.

16. Second Corinthians 4:10–11. Harris, "II Corinthians," 10:343.

Chapter Fourteen: *My Teardrops Dance*

1. Harris, "II Corinthians," 10:315. See also 2 Corinthians 1:3–7; 2:3; 6:10; 7:4, 7, 9, 13, 16; 12:1, 9.

2. Packer, *Knowing God*, 20.

3. Vincent Taylor, *The Epistle to the Romans* (London: Epworth Press, 1955), 14.

4. Romans 2:17–21, 23; 2 Corinthians 1:19–21; 3:21–23. Philippians 3:3, 18–19.

5. Ridderbos, *Paul, An Outline of His Theology*, 141. The difficulty with "exulting" is that some people confuse it with "exalting." We rejoice or *exult* within our hearts. We *exalt* God by lifting him up in worship. Exalting him will cause us to exult, to experience joy.

"Glorying" would be an excellent choice here because of what it conveys of being carried away with rejoicing. We speak of someone exulting, happy in some situation, perhaps in the transparency of love or joy, as being "in her glory." This is the right picture for the joy side of rejoicing, but unfortunately we all know people who seem to "glory in suffering" in a tiring, pathetic way, perhaps "enjoying ill-health." In these two passages in Romans, we will also study "glory" as a noun, so for the most part, we will use the word "rejoicing" rather than its acceptable synonyms.

Another verb available to Paul was *agalliao*; he did not use it; he chose *kauchaomai* for the expression of feelings of joy.

Chapter Fifteen: *Rejoicing in Suffering*

1. Amy Carmichael, *Rose from Brier* (London: SPCK, 1967), xii. The poet, who suffered bedridden through many years of her life, wrote *Rose from Brier*, for the ill, by the ill. She concludes this poem with "O Love of God, do this for me: Maintain a constant victory." We will come back to the topic of what "Christian victory" is, but I think I know Amy well enough from her writings to say that she managed to rejoice in suffering while still processing and expressing human emotion. A plastic smile would have been foreign to her, and she would be ready to admit her own earthenness.

2. Amy Carmichael, "Thou Canst Not Fear Now," in *Toward Jerusalem*, 103.

3. 2 Corinthians 4:7; see also 12:5, 9–10.

4. James 1:2–4; see also 5:11.

5. 1 Peter 1:6–7 (emphasis mine).

6. Steve Bruno, "Fog in the Desert," in *Arizona Highways*, 63, 2, (February 1987): 30.

Chapter Sixteen: *Rejoicing in God*

1. Francis Anderson, *Job, an Introduction and Commentary* (Downers Grove, Ill.: InterVarsity Press, 1976), 72.

2. In Chapter 11, we touched on "proportional valuing," a term given to us by Thomas Oden in *Guilt-Free*. This involves maintaining God and the relationship with him as the ultimate value, and keeping friends and others in their place, so that as limited values they do not become ultimate givers of meaning. Proportional valuing is Oden's term for the right sort of cherishing and perspective. We each need to give thought to this, so that we do not "willfully put God to the test by demanding" the satisfactions that we could "crave." Israel repeatedly made this mistake. And so do I! See Psalm 78:18; Packer, *Knowing God*, 21.

3. Ibid., 22.

4. Ibid.

5. Horatio Spafford, "It Is Well with My Soul," *The Hymnal for Worship and Celebration* (Waco: Word, 1986), 493.

6. Philip Yancey, "How Not To Spell Relief," *Christianity Today* (February 19, 1988): 64.

7. Yancey, *Disappointment with God*, 53. Part 2 in the book is "Making Contact: The Father."

Chapter Seventeen: *R.S.V.P., The Majestic Glory*

1. Dillard, *Pilgrim at Tinker Creek*, 9, 271.

2. Sverre Aalen, "Glory," in *The New International Dictionary of New Testament Theology*, 2:44–45.

3. L. H. Brockington, "The Septuagintal Background to the New Testament Use of Doxa," in *Studies in the Gospels*,

ed. D. E. Nineham (Oxford: Basil Blackwell, 1955), 2–3. Psalms 33:1 and 147:1 tell us that praising God is becoming for the one who follows him. Psalm 96:8, "Ascribe to the LORD the glory due his name." Knowing God brings him glory when we recognize his attributes or characteristics accurately, when we put him in his correct place as God, when we speak, sing, and live out our knowledge. We must not put ourselves or other created things in God's rightful place, exchanging truth for a lie, worshipping and serving "created things rather than the Creator—who is forever praised," Romans 1:18–25. See also John 1:14; Acts 22:11; Isaiah 40:5; Luke 3:4–6; 2 Corinthians 3:7–18; Exodus 34:1–9, 27–35.

4. Cremer, *Biblico-Theological Lexicon* (Edinburgh: Clark, 1895), 208.

5. Karl Barth, *Church Dogmatics*, trans. and ed. Geoffrey Bromiley, (Edinburgh: Clark, 1961), 2–1: 640, 650.

6. 2 Corinthians 3 and 4, particularly 3:18 and 4:16–18. An acquaintance of Katherine's in L'Engle's *A Severed Wasp* says to her, "You are ageless . . . you have lived and suffered and rejoiced, and it's all there, in your face as well as in your [piano] playing, and it is this quality of abundant life which draws me to people," 130.

7. Paul Welter, *How to Help a Friend*, 88–89. In typing "living channels," I inadvertently typed "loving channels," and stumbled onto truth. How can we love others well unless we are fully alive ourselves with all our living channels healthy and operative?

8. Peterson, *Answering God*, 121.

9. Kidner, *Psalms 73–150*, 402. Kidner is commenting on Psalm 113, glory in the heavens (v. 4) and glory in the life of Hannah and her sisters through all the ages (v. 9).

10. Barth, *The Epistle to the Romans*, 305.

11. Peterson, *Answering God*, 127.

12. Ibid.

13. Alan Paton, *For You Departed, A Memoir* (New York: Charles Scribner's Sons, 1969), 135.

Chapter Eighteen: *Smitten by Glory*

1. "The Shorter Catechism," in *The Westminster Confession of Faith* (Edinburgh: The Free Presbyterian Church of Scotland, 1967), 287.

2. D. A. Carson, *The Sermon on the Mount, An Evangelical Exposition of Matthew 5–7* (Grand Rapids, Baker, 1978), 65.

3. Robert Cowley, *The Rulers of Britain* (Chicago: Stonehenge Press, 1982), 140–41.

4. Ibid. Also, Olwen Hedley, *The Queen's Silver Jubilee* (London: Pitkin Pictorials, 1977), 3.

5. Melville Grosvenor and Franc Shor, eds., *This England* (Washington, D.C.: National Geographic Society, 1966), 67.

Epilogue

1. Paton, *For You Departed, A Memoir* (New York: Charles Scribner's Sons, 1969), 62.

2. "God Moves in a Mysterious Way" takes its words from the Scottish Psalter of 1615. It appears with a tune by William Cowper in the *Worship and Service Hymnal* (Chicago: Hope, 1967), 16.

3. The phrase "a severe mercy" originated in a letter from C. S. Lewis to Vanauken. Sheldon Vanauken, *A Severe Mercy* (San Francisco: Harper & Row, 1977), 209.

4. Matthew 6:26; 6:33, paraphrased by Eugene H. Peterson in *The Message* (Colorado Springs: NavPress, 1993), 21. This is the New Testament in Contemporary English.

5. John Main, *The Inner Christ* (London: Darton, Longman and Todd, 1987), 77–78.